Persona and Humor in
Mark Twain's Early Writings

Persona and Humor in
Mark Twain's
Early Writings

Don Florence

University of Missouri Press
Columbia and London

Library of Congress Cataloging-in-Publication Data

Florence, Don, 1955–
    Persona and humor in Mark Twain's early writings /
Don Florence.
        p.   cm.
    Includes bibliographical references and index.
    ISBN 0-8262-1025-2 (alk. paper)
    1. Twain, Mark, 1835–1910—Criticism and interpreta-
tion. 2. Humorous stories, American—History and criticism. 3. Twain, Mark, 1835–1910—Humor. 4. Point of
view (Literature) 5. Comic, The, in literature. 6. Persona (Literature) 7. Narration (Rhetoric) 8. Self in literature. I. Title.
PS1338.F58   1995
818'.409—dc20   95-21080
                                                      CIP

Designer: Kristie Lee
Typesetter: Connell-Zeko Type & Graphics
Printer and Binder: Thomson-Shore, Inc.
Typeface: Caslon 224

*To my mother
and the memory of my father,
and to all those who enjoy
Mark Twain's
humor*

Contents

ᔆᐤᔆ

Acknowledgments

The University of California Press, Berkeley, graciously granted me permission to quote from the following volumes in *The Works of Mark Twain* (series editor Robert H. Hirst): *Early Tales and Sketches,* vols. 1 and 2, edited by Edgar M. Branch and Robert H. Hirst; and *Roughing It,* 1993 edition, edited by Harriet Elinor Smith, Edgar Marquess Branch, Lin Salamo, and Robert Pack Browning.

I would like to thank Bruce Michelson, Leon Chai, and Emily Watts for their many valuable comments on earlier drafts of this work.

I would also like to thank various people at the University of Missouri Press for helping to bring the manuscript to publication: Clair Willcox, Jane Lago, Annette Wenda, Beverly Jarrett, Karen Caplinger, and their respective staffs.

Finally, I would like to thank my uncle Tony Hood for giving me the opportunity to visit some of the places where Samuel Clemens lived and worked in the West.

Persona and Humor in
Mark Twain's Early Writings

1

⌒⊙⌒

The Quest for Persona and Humor

On a recent visit to Hannibal, Missouri, I visited the Mark Twain Cave, or, as it is called in *Tom Sawyer,* McDougal's Cave. The guide dutifully pointed out to me and other wondering tourists the wall where Becky and Tom wrote their names with candle smoke, the place where they first realized they were lost, and the rock beneath which Injun Joe's treasure was buried. A young woman turned to me and said with confusion, "I thought that was all just a story." Many readers are similarly confused by the way Mark Twain confounds illusion and reality in his writings.

Indeed, Twain's writings have often caused readers to blur various categories: fact/fiction, seriousness/humor, Clemens/Twain. Ironically, much Twain criticism is devoted to asserting such distinctions or polarities. Biographical criticism relentlessly tries to track down the man Samuel Clemens behind the writer, persona, and myth known as Mark Twain; such criticism often insists upon asserting a duality or conflict between "Clemens" and "Twain."[1] Moreover, an emphasis on dualities has influenced analyses of the works themselves. Twain criticism frequently focuses on supposed divisions in the works and the persona. Dualities such as primitivism versus sophistication, humor versus satire, and tenderfoot versus old-timer abound in Twain scholarship. Furthermore, many studies attempt to show how the supposedly cheerful Mark Twain of the early works evolves into the supposedly nihilistic Mark Twain in later works.[2]

To some extent, Twain's writings do enact such polarities, and there is value in studies that try to delineate relationships between man and persona. This study, however, is concerned almost exclusively with Twain as the controller of his works, a personality much

1

more complex than dualities can suggest. When I refer to Mark Twain, I mean the literary personality who shapes and dominates a given work—the image we have of the author based on our reading of that work. That is, my use of "Mark Twain" is akin to Wayne C. Booth's concept of the "implied author" or the author-created "second self"—a literary personality that is both in and behind a given work and normally includes a narrative voice, though it goes beyond any particular narrator.[3] Or, to adopt the terminology of the Geneva School of phenomenological criticism, Mark Twain is the mind that we sense both governing a work and expressing itself through that work—the literary mode of thought, if you will, that Samuel Clemens entered into whenever he sat down to write. In short, Mark Twain is what Samuel Clemens becomes—and perhaps in some ways fundamentally *is*—as a writer and persona: it is the way we are induced to conceptualize him. Mark Twain's persona—or Mark Twain *as* a persona—is the basic way Twain is projected in a given work; it is how we know him as a literary consciousness. To a large extent, we construct the implied author Mark Twain, the metaphysical entity behind and creator of a given work, through his manifestation as narrator and character (persona) in that work. We impute motives, strategies, and characteristics to this implied author to account for the work and his presence as a persona in it. Although there are occasional epistemological and semantic abysses, in general Mark Twain "has" or "is" a persona in much the same way that I "have" or "am" a personality: my personality is what is knowable or identifiable about "me." For most practical purposes, the name *Mark Twain* and the term *persona* may be used interchangeably when discussing a particular work. The persona is what we "recognize" as the implied author, Mark Twain.

Granted, we may not always strictly equate persona with implied author. Sometimes the persona may be seen as a deliberate pose, a game played by the implied author, especially when Twain presents himself as, say, a fool or engages in obvious exaggerations. At such times we may conceive of the implied author as a more reasonable or "toned down" version of the persona. Complicating our reading further, Twain may vary in voice or role from one sentence to the next in his most sophisticated narratives. At one moment "persona" and "implied author" may seem identical, whereas in the next moment we may sense a gap. Nevertheless, our conception of the implied author is normally drawn from his expression as a persona; we consider both as Twain.

In general, Twain's early writings are presented as "narrative histories" that direct us to the implied author behind them. Interweaving fact and fiction, these narratives are fictive truths, or better yet, true fictions. They are presented as the authentic records of Mark Twain. His persona—often as both the protagonist *and* the narrator—is offered in a given work as an aspect of Mark Twain, or as a moment in his "life." Sometimes Mark Twain as a persona may be narrowly confined, especially in a brief journalistic piece; elsewhere he may be multifaceted, as in a sophisticated narrative like *The Innocents Abroad*. Regardless, our psychological experience in reading a Twain narrative is likely to be that we are reading a history of Mark Twain. We may be sufficiently informed to realize that such history often may not recount the life of Samuel Clemens; but, if we accept the narrative on its own terms, if we are true to the implicit contract between author and reader, then the narrative becomes part of the record of Mark Twain. Taken together, such narratives give us the fascinating story of a larger-than-life creation.

The fact that the author we conceptualize is Mark Twain, not Samuel Clemens, helps explain why it is so difficult for biographers to track down Samuel Clemens through the writings of Mark Twain. Though works such as *The Innocents Abroad* and *Roughing It* originate at least partly in the experiences of Samuel Clemens, they are transmuted into narrative fiction about this other somebody named Mark Twain. Narrative, persona, and implied author are all linguistic constructs: we are persuaded to participate in the construction of the imaginary history of an imaginary being, Mark Twain, and to compose him at various periods in that history.

Even if we turn to letters, notebooks, and dictated reminiscences, we are presented with personae and authorial images that suggest Mark Twain, not Samuel Clemens. For example, in the purportedly autobiographical dictations set down in Clemens's late years, whimsy and playful exaggerations suggest more fiction and self-creation, not history—we hear the story and voice of Mark Twain, not Samuel Clemens. In the letters and notebooks, too, one senses Mark Twain much more than a flesh-and-blood man. In the process of writing, the literary consciousness, showman, and persona known as Mark Twain emerges—an intricate sensibility, a mode of thinking and expressing, a self-formed literary being. From the narratives we also construct Mark Twain, this "being" who is finally more than just an abstract or disembodied voice—a being who has become a cultural icon and stands on his own as a clearly recognizable personality, as evidenced by films such as *The Adventures of Mark Twain* and a plethora of other popular accounts of his life and times.

It's tempting to think of Mark Twain as a mask of Samuel Clemens, but that notion is misleading if we consider a mask as something static, something donned and doffed at will. There may be a great deal of Samuel Clemens in Mark Twain, though just how much we may never determine. Just as his narratives are often built on fictionalized facts, perhaps Mark Twain is an aspect, mode of thought, or "fact" of Samuel Clemens that has been fictionalized (dramatized). Like the fiction that illuminates a fact, like the birthmark in Hawthorne's "The Birthmark" that cannot be removed without destroying its possessor, perhaps Mark Twain is a birthmark, or rather a "thought-mark" of Samuel Clemens, essential to his expression. In any event, though Mark Twain may be ultimately a mirage, a phony, he may be, like Holly Golightly, a *real* phony, truly expressive of puzzling—and comic—questions about the world and the self. Perhaps the best analogy is offered by *No. 44, The Mysterious Stranger:* Clemens is the "waking self"; Twain is the fascinating "dream self," the creator, narrator, and protagonist of a wealth of dream adventures. Perhaps Mark Twain is Samuel Clemens rendered fantastic and glorious—or at least humorous, even in his "darkest" narratives. As long as we stay within those narratives, concerning ourselves with persona and implied author, we need not be concerned with what Samuel Clemens was "really" like—though we may occasionally wish to speculate.

While Twain's narratives encourage us to accept him and his adventures on their own terms, sometimes they also prompt us to question what we read. Twain's playfulness, capacity for change, and penchant for hoax may, at times, induce us to wonder in what manner a particular narrative is to be regarded. In other words, even within the context of a narrative we may be puzzled; Twain's narratives sometimes delight in undercutting themselves.

Moreover, while these narratives present Mark Twain and his (usually invented) "experiences," they nonetheless are, in a sense, often reportorial, pointing "outward." That is, they present places—the Old World, the American West—for our consideration. These places may ultimately serve as settings or backdrops for Mark Twain's comic revels, but we may still wonder just how accurately these settings are rendered. Again, Twain may prompt us to various responses: at times we may accept his descriptions, at other times we may question them. Twain seems sometimes a reporter, sometimes a dreamer. On occasion we may question whether there even *is* an "outside" or objective world (that is, a world open to *anyone*'s factual portrayal). In short, just as Melville leads us to contemplate the whiteness of the whale in *Moby-Dick* and Poe confronts us with a snow-white "shrouded human figure" in *Pym,* Twain brings us to face a blankness, an epistemological void. Twain's method is comic rather than melodramatic or horrific; nevertheless, by encouraging us to ponder Mark Twain, his adventures, and his world, he prompts us, at least occasionally, to philosophical speculation. We may recall the mind-world or subject-object problems posed in epistemology: we are presented with a mind, Mark Twain, of whose narrative "reality" we are assured yet whose changeability may puzzle (and delight) us. We may laughingly wonder how to consider this mind, its experiences, and its relationship to any "outside" world; and thereby we may find some parallels to our own situation, as we narrate our own existence to ourselves. Twain suggests how complex and indeterminate is the relationship between mind and object, narrative and world.

Be that as it may, we enjoy Mark Twain's adventures and forms for their own sake. Mark Twain may manifest himself in various ways in a particular work, including the narrator's voice and the voices of those characters who seem to be projecting, at least partly, the implied author's views and consciousness. In his early writings Twain favors first-person narrations; thus, he may be generally identified with these narrator-protagonists, these narrative voices. Each role or voice is, in a sense, an incarnation of Mark Twain—a particular self that Twain may become, or express himself as, for the purposes of that narrative. As implied author, Twain is the inventive capacity, the creator of all these voices and selves, the containing envelope for all these particularities and aspects of himself. He gives a measure of continuity to these various narratives and lets us speak of Mark Twain generally, instead of just the Mark Twain of *The Innocents Abroad* or the Mark Twain of *Roughing It*. He lets us talk about the voices or personae *of* Mark Twain.

With each new narrative, Mark Twain is expressed in increasingly complex ways. Indeed, with the completion of *Roughing It* Mark Twain has evolved into a multifaceted personality a bit like Harry Haller in Hesse's *Steppenwolf*: a "Magic Theater" of seemingly innumerable dramatic and creative possibilities, a domain for a medley of "selves" or potentialities. Like Haller, Twain becomes a fluid consciousness that delights in dissolving distinctions, staging scenes that are simultaneously realistic and surrealistic, and expressing an array of attitudes and tones.

The way to enter the Magic Theater of Haller's mind is through humor: Haller laughs at an image of himself in a mirror, shattering his self-image into many pieces. Thereby freed from restrictive notions of self, identity, and reality, Haller is able to enter the Magic Theater and play with the multiplicities and possibilities of his mind. So, too, does Mark Twain use humor as a liberating and volatilizing power, a comic impulse that recasts experience, world, and self into new forms. Humor is an awareness of the incongruities and multiplicities in world and self—and it is also a playful willingness to use this awareness to reshape, or view anew, world and self.

That humor depends upon a playful and pleasant awareness of incongruities and offers liberation is not a new idea, of course. In his essay "Humour" (1927) Sigmund Freud noted that "humour has something liberating about it, but it also has something of grandeur and elevation." He added: "The grandeur of it clearly lies in the triumph of narcissism, the victorious assertion of the ego's invulnerability. The ego refuses to be distressed by the provocations of reality, to let itself be compelled to suffer. It insists that it cannot be affected by the traumas of the external world; it shows, in fact, that such traumas are no more than occasions for it to gain pleasure." Similarly, Norman N. Holland contends that "if we perceive a sudden, playful incongruity that gratifies conscious and unconscious wishes and defeats conscious and unconscious fears to give a feeling of liberation, then we laugh."[4] Where I differ from this well-established psychoanalytic line is in my emphasis on humor as offering volatility and creativity. Rather than seeing humor as simply reassuring the ego (or re-creating one's identity theme, as Holland would have it), I see humor—Mark Twain's humor, at any rate—as offering fluidity, expansion, and adventure, thereby engendering *new* images of world and self.

Within Twain's comic narratives, then, the world may be created afresh. By refusing to let experience dictate his role, by laughing at everyday distinctions, conventions, and fixities—by rejecting, in short, anything that might fixate him—Twain asserts through humor the variability and inventiveness that make up his persona. Humor's ability to uncover life's lurking disjunctions, ambiguities, and absurdities—life's general "messiness"—lets Twain suggest that neither world nor self is so knowable, stable, or determined as generally assumed. By denying a fixed and wholly objective world, humor frees the mind to shift ideas and perspectives easily, to revel in the exposure and creation of the absurd. Humor dissolves appearances, revealing the hidden formlessness of life in order to let the mind laughingly manufacture its own forms.

In some respects Twain uses humor the way Socrates used irony. As Søren Kierkegaard pointed out in *The Concept of Irony,* Socrates (and later, Hegel) used irony as "infinite absolute negativity." Kierkegaard explained: "Here, then, we see irony in all its divine infinitude, which allows nothing whatever to endure." Constantly changing ironic masks, Socrates exposed human foibles and pretenses—especially the pretense that we really know the world and ourselves. Such a "clearing away" of false knowledge, such a brushfire among the thickets of illusion and conceit, enabled Socrates to indicate what was hitherto concealed: the sphere of the Absolute, the "really real" realm of Ideas.[5]

Twain's humor also engages in this ironic dissolution of conventionally accepted "reality." As burlesque, hoax, linguistic game, or satire, Twain's multiform humor often denies the reality principle, denies the world as an objective and imposing force, and denies the power of circumstance to fix, define, or limit. Like philosophical ironists from Socrates to Kierkegaard, Twain uses his ironic humor to suggest that life is more illusory and protean than commonly believed. Kierkegaard's observation that irony grants seemingly infinite opportunities for playing with the world may be aptly applied to Twain's humorous reshaping of experience.[6]

Twain differs from this long tradition of metaphysical irony in his refusal to espouse any absolute truth, any noumenal realm behind the phenomenal world. Whereas ironists like Socrates, Hegel, and Kierkegaard used irony to strip away veils of appearances to reveal Truth, Twain's humor strips away veils in order to suggest further veils, with existence as a shadow show. Indeed, Twain loves to destroy illusions *and* to reveal—or create—new ones in their stead. If there is anything "real" in Twain's writings, it is his creative consciousness, his power to make his own world. Absolute reality is the literary mind itself: Mark Twain as creator of selves, hoaxes, and illusions.

It is Mark Twain's humor, his exuberant transforming of experience, that reveals him to us; humor simultaneously creates, sustains, and expresses his versatile persona. As an active agent for change, humor lets him alter subject and stance at will; it grants him power and freedom. Even when narrating humiliations, he asserts through laughter his invulnerability to painful experiences, his liberation from restraint. By using the creative quirkiness of humor he links moods, events, and people in fresh and unexpected ways, presenting a world that he wants or at least can control. Mark Twain's humor is his liberating power to refashion life according to the fluidity of his own mind; it is his freedom from definitions, concrete events, and causalities. It suggests that beneath the apparently solid world is a world of sportive absurdity, a protean, unfathomable world open to continual remaking. This revelation empowers Twain to be likewise protean, creative, absurd—to remake the world and his persona within comic narrative. By volatilizing and reinventing the world, Twain's humor engenders a volatile, evolving persona. The process is interactive: By changing himself, Mark Twain changes his relationship with the world, and his images of it.

Moreover, humor is mainly verbal; it recasts world and self through language, suggesting that language itself is inherently unstable and that verbal representations of life are illusory.[7] Because language is how the mind primarily conceptualizes the world and the self, such conceptualizations are naturally subject to distortion and transformation. By underscoring and magnifying the instabilities of language and thought, humor renders the world and the self protean.

Through humor Twain implies that word and world are much more unsettled than we ordinarily realize. Ideas, categories, and distinctions—including those between the serious and the nonsensical—may dissolve easily in the flux of the humorous mind. In Twain, absurdity may penetrate the most serious subject; nonsense may commingle with the numinous.

Because Mark Twain is created and presented by the flux of comic language, he becomes as variable as the world he presents. Like that world, he becomes a protean linguistic phenomenon. As persona, as voice and protagonist in his narratives, he becomes as versatile as the comic words that create him. In short, Mark Twain, his writings, and his world all depend upon the versatility of his humor.

The extreme versatility of Twain's humor helps suggest why conventional explanations of humor or laughter often fail when applied to Twain's writing. For instance, Henri Bergson's theory that we laugh at a lack of emotion and "mechanical inelasticity" (or "something mechanical encrusted on the living") may not explain why we laugh at Twain's humorous narratives, which often are emotionally charged and depend on flexibility, not inflexibility.[8] To take a quick example, Twain's hilarious portrayal of himself in *The Innocents Abroad* as weeping over the alleged grave of Adam is implicitly charged with contempt for superstition and plays brilliantly and agilely off the Adam myth. Scholars such as James M. Cox and Bruce Michelson note that Twain's humor tends to be good-natured play, an act of spontaneous, childlike creation.

In *Homo Ludens* Johan Huizinga defines play as a game with its own rules, play area, and rituals; role-playing is a prominent form of play. Clearly Twain's humor often depends upon roles, masks, and games; play theory is especially applicable to *Tom Sawyer* and similar works, and much of Twain's humor can be broadly characterized as "playful." Furthermore, whether it is Cox emphasizing Freud's pleasure principle or Michelson emphasizing a sense of fun, such critics are right to point to the sheer enjoyment found in Twain's humor—a seemingly obvious fact that is occasionally overlooked in the all-too-serious world of literary scholarship.

But a preoccupation with play per se will not capture the full range of Twain's humor and persona, unless we recognize that Twain's "play" is frequently not ritualistic, not concerned with rules (which

Twain tends to dissolve as soon as he makes them), and not entirely devoted to pleasure or fun. A surcharge of emotion and ideas often gives his humor a forcefulness, an ability to break down and rearrange our conceptions of the world, that is not found in play alone. For Twain, "play" is the humorous transformation of life—including all of its "rules"—into fantasy, where concepts may be set in startlingly new contexts. Moreover, Twain often gives a sense of movement, even transcendence, that is not captured by play theory, though Huizinga does include a vague feeling of "rapture" as among the "elements proper to play."[9]

At its best, Mark Twain's humor is both a resilient response to an incongruous world and a surmounting of that world through his ability to make his own imaginative worlds. Twain fashions worlds full of exaggerations, linguistic revels, and radically altered perceptions. The product is humorous "fantasy"; yet, as created mental realms, Twain's worlds are also "real," often containing important insights into the way in which the mind produces its sense of existence. To put it another way, Twain's humor offers both paradox and transcendence: his humor points to—and even exaggerates—the absurdities, contradictions, and illusions inherent in life, yet suggests that one can rise above life's limitations through a humorous consciousness that manufactures its own sense of life, its own place.[10] In a world of illusions one can at least make one's *own* illusions—fantasies that are created rather than accepted, fantasies that at least have the "reality" of one's own mind. In Twain's narratives, conventional distinctions between illusion and reality are often dissolved in his expanding consciousness. Through humor Mark Twain becomes a personality whose essence or meaning rests not upon the accidents of an external world but upon itself—a literary consciousness that creates itself and is its own world.

This is not to say that the man Samuel Clemens did not face various exigencies. His literary career, especially in its early stages, was influenced by market pressures, the demands of journalism, and awareness of his various audiences. Nevertheless, Mark Twain increasingly presents himself in his narratives as a literary personality who, however fallible or self-disparaging, is largely self-made: a multifaceted, inventive (and invented) being that humorously observes—and shapes—his world. Furthermore, as he gains characteristics, stances, and voices, Mark Twain develops his own dynamic, his own motive force, which will lead him (albeit in willful and meandering ways!) through future narratives. In short, although Mark Twain obviously depends upon the experiences of Samuel Clemens, he also becomes a self-defined persona inhabiting and reveling in various literary realms.

Granted, Twain uses humor to reveal incongruities and frustrations inherent in life and in oneself—the dilemma of a sensitive being who discovers that the world is not always set up for his accommodation and that he is not always set up for his accommodation, either. Torn by conflicting desires, one needs imaginative renewal and a balance of perspectives. Twain's humor confers needed reassurance and control. It matters little if the material of humor is often discomfort, deception, or human frailty, so long as the sense of mastery remains. The inventive capability of comic narrative suggests that the locus of meaning, of reality, ultimately resides in the literary mind itself, not in the external world; it is this exuberant sense of power to reshape or resignify oneself and one's world that grants the humorist his aura of transcendence. It is not transcendence in the sense of ascending into some immortal, Platonic realm of the Absolute; rather, it is transcendence over the fears, stupidities, and general dullness of everyday life. By denying the power of the concrete world to make and define him, Mark Twain asserts his ability to form models of life—and of himself—according to his own humorous imagination.[11]

Befitting the protean persona it helps to make and empower, Mark Twain's humor is kaleidoscopic, embodying frontier fantasy, burlesque, anecdote, cracker-box philosophy, hoax, satire, irony, literary comedy and linguistic games, and absurdity—all methods of recasting or restaging the world according to stage manager Twain's theater of moods and ideas. Despite its extreme range, Twain's humor is, at its best, a harmonizing force, balancing illusion against illusion, model against model, making a comic symphony (if occasionally out of tune) of his variegated persona. Twain presents humor as a peculiar form of music, as opposed to the discord of tragedy; the humorist delights in each tone of life and imagination. Humor lets him move almost musically from one view, role, or "self" to the next, enjoying each in its turn. Whereas tragedy tends to fixate on one problem or perspective, Twain's humor moves through a medley of moods and motifs. Even in the form of hoax or satire, jarring our beliefs and pretensions, his humor happily expresses the power of persona, his delight in playing with ideas.

In his desire to make humor, to exercise mastery, Twain often destroys models of reality that others take for granted. He frequently transgresses ordinary boundaries, habits of thought, and conceptions of life; his humor is often manifest in dreams or dreamlike scenes, power fantasies, and a persistent sense of wild, if troubled, freedom. As he constructs models of life to suit his own humorous will, Twain develops his persona. Even when exposing life's disappointments and his own flaws, Twain implicitly asserts his power to reflect upon and surmount them, to give birth to yet other—and better—selves. Ultimately Twain's humor is not of the world but of himself—a reflection of his own versatile mind, playing at increasingly higher levels. He uses humor to remake language, narrative, history, and even basic conceptions of reality and identity. He subsumes and shapes more and more of the world, making fresh associations and images. He makes humor out of the very nature of consciousness. For Twain, to think is to be humorous, to be playfully cognizant of the fluidity, nonsense, and creativity that is consciousness. Through humor Twain dreams better worlds and better selves.

Twain achieves this fluidity of persona and humor over the course of his early writings, and the basic "presence" of Mark Twain is evident with the publication of *Roughing It* in 1872.[12] In contradistinction to those critics who see the later Twain as dramatically opposed to an earlier persona, I consider that Twain achieved fluidity as a literary self by 1872 and maintained it throughout his career. Ironic, skeptical, and volatile, a veritable play of voices, Mark Twain shows from first to last his sense of the world and the self in flux—and he also shows his determination to explore and play with that flux to the fullest. Even the so-called dark Twain of *Connecticut Yankee* and later writings is in some ways a deepening of the persona and views that take shape in the early writings; often the differences are more in degree than in kind.[13] Twain challenges concepts and conventions: he explores subjects from sundry perspectives; takes ideas to their logical—or illogical—extremes; extrapolates from previous motifs; multiplies the devices and uses of his humor; and exerts his multiform personality against confining circumstances. In some ways his greatest consistency is his fluidity—the fact that to be Mark Twain is to be forever restless, forever engaged dramatically with world and self.

His fluidity is one reason Twain is notoriously difficult to write about. Indeed, though one cannot help speaking of an "I," an identity in a given work, such expressions are misleading if one considers identity to imply strict unity or integration. Such terms connote fixity; though there are occasional tendencies toward fixity in Twain's work, most of his writing evokes a sense of the protean, an evolution and play of persona. One key trend of Twain's early career, from his western journalism through *The Innocents Abroad* to *Roughing It,* is his development into a versatile, humorous persona who can surmount the polarities and disjunctions of life. Through humor Twain gradually evolves into a persona who can express almost any viewpoint fully. Because humor lets him penetrate and subvert illusions and supposed fixities, because humor denies the absoluteness or immutability of virtually any given idea, relationship, or convention, Twain is free to alter his personality and reactions to the world without seeming disastrously inconsistent. Customarily, the self and the surrounding world are defined by the relationships established with people, places, and ideas—a network of fairly stable links. Mark Twain's humor, however, often breaks links and ideas, forming new ones in their place. The same object—for example, an alleged Christian "relic" in *The Innocents Abroad*—may at one moment elicit scorn; the next, amused tolerance. What changes is not the object itself but Twain's mode of perceiving it: his way of presenting it, himself, and his relationship to it. A variable humor permits a variable persona, which in turn permits variable perceptions—and yet more variable humor. Mark Twain becomes an elastic envelope for a protean play of humorous responses.

In his early western journalism, Twain experiments with one perspective after another, though he is often limited to one basic viewpoint per piece because of the brevity of the pieces and journalistic confinements. He develops an assortment of perspectives and humorous techniques without yet developing into a persona sufficiently flexible to encompass them easily. In *The Innocents Abroad* Twain grapples with problems posed by the confrontation of the

New World with the Old World, the present with the past. Caught in epistemological quandaries, he extends and volatilizes both persona and humor, trying to project a narrative consciousness that will not be overwhelmed by such problems. To a large extent he is successful—the attentive reader will recognize that the narrative is ultimately more about Mark Twain, the developing persona, than about the Old World. Nevertheless, although Twain shows himself as considerably more intricate and inclusive than in his early western writings, he is still not always able to master his subject matter, not always able to re-create the Old World to fit the demands of humor and narrative. It is only in *Roughing It* that Mark Twain as persona emerges truly victorious, albeit at a price. In *Roughing It* Mark Twain becomes the supreme shaping force of the narrative, the arbiter of what meaning is, of what reality is, of what humor is. He is as complex and fluid as the confusing world he confronts; he makes use of the world's incongruities and illusions, rather than becoming their victim. In short, he controls his narrative and his world, exulting in his ability to conjure images, illusions, and new perspectives at will.

There is, however, the danger of becoming too volatile and thus evaporating. In his humorous versatility and self-sufficiency Twain may rise superior to the world of empirical events only to become "pinnacled dim in the intense inane," alone and abstracted into the void. There is the danger that a wholly fluid persona may be so nonintegral as to dissolve. Though Twain needs to be flexible, he must not rupture the elastic envelope of his persona; he must not destroy the sense of a locus or presence (however protean) in his work. Though he is generated primarily by humor, Twain must be more than just a series of discrete humorous responses to life. It is not just a question of Mark Twain having secondary dimensions (the sentimental, the romantic, the moral) that sometimes are and sometimes are not subsumed by his comic impulse. Even if we were to identify Twain entirely with his humorous impulse, we need to see him as not just made by that humor but as also *using* that humor to transform world and self, to assert himself as a creative presence. Recall one paradox of humor: While revealing the incongruities, frustrations, and absurdities of life that one is vulnerable to, humor also offers a sense of liberation and transcendence over such empirical confinements. Humor is freedom, escape from experience through the rearrangement of that experience. Mark Twain's multiple "selves" or humorous avatars permit such transcendence or escape—but only if there is *something* (however nebulous) to escape *to*. If he surmounts circumstance through and into his humorous mind, that mind must be a distinct "place." Though his fluidity and multiplicities demand that he resist fixity and confining concepts of unity, he must still convey a sense of presence. Behind all the voices and incarnations there must be something we sense as Mark Twain: detached from, inviolable to, and transcendent beyond all situations and roles that he makes and controls through his narration and from which he can liberate himself whenever he desires. The persona must have some identity, some underlying sustainment; as readers, we must have some sense of Mark Twain, the persona and implied author, as a being, a mind, if his narratives are not to lapse into chaos before us. If Mark Twain disappears into chaos or dadaistic disruption, then humor and freedom also disappear. Behind Mark Twain's humorous cogitations must be a humorous cogitator.

The issue runs yet deeper. Though all fictive writing may be deemed a recasting of the world, we've seen that this point holds especially true for humorous writing. There may be nothing humorous about human life: it seems to be a protracted struggle for significance by a slowly dying being. We may recall Yeats's lament in "Sailing to Byzantium":

> Consume my heart away; sick with desire
> And fastened to a dying animal
> It knows not what it is. . . .

Yeats sought escape into the "artifice of eternity" through his poetic art; Twain sought escape into the forever protean, the forever vital, through his humor. It is in the subjective, in the free and creative mind, that humor may be found. Humor strives to make the world subservient to the mind; indeed, the humorist strives to assert that his humor, his mind, is the measure or center of reality, that humorous consciousness is what finally matters. In humor, tone is all-important: for something to be seen as comic, it must first be remade, dipped and coated in humorous thought. For something to be funny, it must enter the humorous world of the humorous mind. Should that world shatter, should that mind (here, Mark Twain) disintegrate, should the reader no longer sense a manufacturing and controlling presence, a force for humor in the work, then the writing lapses into the banality of ordinary existence.

To prevent this lapse, Mark Twain must be a distinct, if protean, presence in his writings. From his fragmented and often tentative early pieces, through the complex confrontations of *The Innocents Abroad,* to the fantasy- and myth-making of *Roughing It,* Twain renders his humor increasingly forceful, imaginative, and flexible, both developing and asserting himself as a persona. A humor that sports and undercuts and assumes new perspectives, a vigorous persona who alters in form—such is the achievement in these early narratives. Indeed, the writings through *Roughing It* form a distinct, self-contained movement that takes Twain as far as he is to go in a certain direction; namely, that of a variable, inclusive personality who uses the plasticity of humor to unsettle our notions of a fixed world.

In later narratives Mark Twain assumes more distinct forms; he presents a more defined locus for his literary consciousness and offers a more pronounced social engagement for his humor; he forgoes some freedom and flexibility as persona/implied author to attain greater stability and communal identification. The writings after *Roughing It* thus represent some modification in Twain's development. Characters such as Tom Sawyer and Huck Finn may be seen as aspects or particular "projections" of the underlying literary personality, as that personality tries to engage more concretely with the world. I would contend, though, that as befits the multiform literary personality behind these characters, both Tom Sawyer and Huck Finn are considerably more complex and variable than has perhaps been generally acknowledged. Although Mark Twain is not directly and flamboyantly present in many of his later writings the way he is (as an "I") in his early writings, he is still there as implied author, as a humorous literary consciousness shaping the world his characters inhabit. In short, the Mark Twain of the later writings is made possible by the Mark Twain of the early writings. Mark Twain gradually evolves into a presence that is both transcendent and earthy, abstract and concrete, supreme and communal—a personality that has both fluidity and form. At the end of *Steppenwolf* Harry Haller aspires to the cold, ethereal laughter of the Immortals; Mark Twain offers laughter that is equally transcendent, equally immune to life's pain and confusion, yet warmer.

2

✃

A Washoe Zephyr

When he came to Nevada Territory (nicknamed Washoe) in 1861, Samuel Clemens encountered the ironically named Washoe Zephyr: "At sunset yesterday, the wind commenced blowing after a fashion to which a typhoon is mere nonsense, and in a short time the face of heaven was obscured by vast clouds of dust all spangled over with lumber, and shingles, and dogs and things."[1] Mark Twain would elaborate upon this description in a brilliantly humorous passage in *Roughing It*, but at the time Samuel Clemens may have felt dizzied by such swirling gusts. Indeed, the swirls were not just of the wind but probably also of his soul: his family background, travels, and occupations may have left him with turmoil, for which the Washoe Zephyr would be a fitting symbol. His father died when Clemens was eleven; his younger brother, Henry, died at the age of twenty in a steamboat explosion; and his older brother, Orion, recently appointed Secretary of Nevada Territory, was already showing the moody shifting of interests, religious beliefs, political affiliations, and occupations that would plague him—and bewilder Sam—for many years to come. Mark Twain would present himself as an untraveled innocent at the beginning of *Roughing It;* but Samuel Clemens had been east when he was seventeen, visiting and working in Philadelphia, Washington, and New York, and a few years later he had traveled up the Ohio River, working in Cincinnati for a while, before going back down the Ohio and down the Mississippi to New Orleans. Clemens had worked as a journeyman printer and had learned, under Horace Bixby, to be a steamboat pilot on the Mississippi, where he later claimed that he had met every type of person imaginable. When the Civil War closed the Mississippi, he spent a few weeks as a volunteer in the

Marion County Rangers, a Confederate force, and then left for Nevada Territory with Orion. His family tragedies, travels, and "variegated" (a favorite Twain word) experiences may have left Clemens feeling that life in general, not just in Nevada Territory, was beset by strong and contradictory winds.[2]

He came to a land that was chaotic, violent, and unformed. Nevada Territory, especially Virginia City with its famous Comstock Lode, was a melting pot for many sorts of people, including desperadoes. Mining speculation, backed by the banking and mining concerns of San Francisco, was rampant. At nearly every turn Clemens was to encounter greed, pipe dreams, murders, deception, wild exaggerations, and a strange unreality that bespoke both dream and nightmare—all set in the vast West, which was both infinitely promising and infinitely threatening, another world entirely with its alien landscape.[3] Later he would find San Francisco a puzzling mixture of beauty and corruption, sophistication and barbarism; still later he would respond to the Sandwich Islands as Melville had responded to the Marquesas, seeing the tropical islands as a peculiar paradise whose lush vegetation could not entirely hide a legacy of darkness and cannibalism, a place that was both a retreat and a trap, and one that would be both blessed and cursed by the coming of commerce, missionaries, and Western civilization. These bewildering experiences help form the variegated literary consciousness known as Mark Twain. Twain takes the vertiginous life of Clemens and fashions it into humorous narrative. The discordant facts of Clemens become the playful fictions of Twain.

Writing about Nevada Territory, San Francisco, and the Sandwich Islands, Twain indicates how hard it is to arrive at an assessment of these strange places. He shows that hoaxes, illusions, and discrepancies abound, suggesting the lack of a stable frame of reference. The American West and Sandwich Islands pose for Twain much the same problems that Europe and the Orient will later present him in *The Innocents Abroad:* how to make sense out of that which resists interpretation and pattern. As Twain presents the West, it is fraught with ironies and fantasies. An uninhibited land given to dreams that dissolve categories and conventional notions of "truth," the West places a premium on resiliency and flexibility. Twain indicates that, despite its disappointments and illusions, the

West stresses democratic notions of social mobility: the openness and freedom seem to offer a chance to become whomever one wants, to do whatever one can. In short, the West emphasizes changeability by encouraging one to render the world and the self protean, to forsake set ideas such as "reality" or "identity." As Twain presents contradictions and variability, he evolves into a versatile persona; he becomes able to convert the void of the West, empty of secure standards of knowledge or culture, into a playground for his comic fantasies. Through his hoaxes, burlesques, tall tales, and linguistic games, Twain begins to remake the West into a theater for his comic self-dramatization.

The evolution of Twain in the West passes through several stages. He tests his versatility and capacity for fantasy-making by transmuting the incongruities and hoaxes of the West—its endless confidence games—into his own playful fantasies. In a land of flux and dreams that renounces the fixed forms of the East and Europe, he shows his ability to eschew rigidity, distinctions, and objective fact. He delights in the freewheeling, childlike nature of westerners—a quality suggestive of both innocence and trickery. He develops himself as a paradoxically naïve trickster figure, one who can use his seemingly innocent humor to poke fun at the West and to fool his readers into accepting *his* fantasies and games. Through the freedom of humorous language, Twain—simultaneously the creator and product of that language—frequently overcomes pain, disappointment, and anything that might confine him. Twain tends to become as multiform and mobile as the West itself.

Such mobility, though, may also imply extreme instability, a lack of integrity; at times Twain seeks structure, if only in dualities. He experiments with a split in his persona between romanticism and realism, as exemplified by the Twain-Brown dualism in the Sandwich Islands material. Such experiments do not always fully express Twain and his humor, and thus he begins developing into a persona who can go beyond dualities, artificial distinctions, and preoccupation with structure. His humor volatilizes him into a fluidity that escapes categories and conventions. In presenting a baffling world, Twain refuses to be pinned down or puzzled for long. In changefulness lies safety, for then he cannot be forced by the world into a specific role. It is Twain's humor, his play of attitudes and tones, his refusal to be committed to (or entrapped by) any one perspective, that renders him so protean. His humor recasts experience so as to give him power over that experience; he transforms the often traumatic experiences of Clemens into the comic forays of Twain. Twain's versatile humor lets him manufacture a narrative that is not "fixed" or determined by misfortune. Yet Twain needs to be variable without disintegrating into comic disarray. He needs to be fluid without being anarchic, to be kaleidoscopic without being chaotic.

Twain begins to evolve into a persona who has both plasticity and purpose. Suggesting the changeability not only of the West but also of language, thought, and even the self, Twain begins presenting himself as a being—or rather, a humorous linguistic process—that transcends the West, ordinary notions of identity, and even the supposedly fixed past. He plays with the meanings of words and thereby suggests that he may also play with his sense of "reality"—and with his sense of what it means to be an "I." Free to remake word, world, and self, Twain implies that ultimately he may surmount almost any limitation or definition. Within the realm of humorous discourse he suggests that there is no final "truth" or form to the world or self—there is only his play of language and attitudes. Unfettered, he may transform—and transcend—himself and the West, including its incongruities, through his comic confidence games.

Perhaps the most basic western incongruity is that between expectation and reality, especially between anticipation of wealth and subsequent poverty. Not surprisingly, bewilderment underlies many of Twain's ironies and hoaxes, bewilderment familiar to impoverished miners of Nevada Territory and California, who often had reason to feel that the entire West was a hoax. In addition, Twain dramatizes discrepancies in his views of nature, cultural conflicts between West and East, and contradictions in human nature. He uses comic irony to highlight incongruities; he uses humor and satire, often as burlesque, to express tolerance or scorn, or both, for the West's confusions and disappointments.

Whereas it is customary to consider humor as good-natured acceptance and satire as normative and corrective, such distinctions often break down in Twain, who delights in shifting attitudes, values, and forms, and who frequently manages to be both corrective and accepting of the world. Much of Twain's work is satiric in that it criticizes human folly; yet the sense of fun, the comic tone, is rarely lost. Twain's satire often blends into his humor because it is lambent, instead of an intense light focused on human foibles. Traditional satire implies moral fixity, a commitment to a given solution (often "right reason"), whereas Twain shows the world's stupidities in a playful spirit and is too protean in his imaginative rendering of life to be committed for long to any one perspective. Twain suggests there is no "right" order, no "standard" referent, to which one can appeal. Indeed, in his variability Twain satirizes much traditional satire, undermining the rigidity that too often besets the determined satirist. Satire and humor do have as a common denominator a focus on life's ludicrousness; Twain, unlike most satirists, delights in this ludicrousness, even when criticizing its manifestation in particular human frailties. In other words, though he recognizes and condemns certain forms that ridiculousness may assume (ranging from prejudice to war), Twain accepts and even revels in life's basic absurdity. Even in his most intent satire he suggests that major flaws in human nature—and in the conditions of existence—aren't really remediable anyway, so one might as well enjoy the nonsense of it all. In its illustration of life's changeability, absurdity, and relativity, Twain's satire is enveloped entirely within his humor.

Satiric and humorous, Twain's presentation of the West's incongruities is part of a long American literary tradition. It has become a truism that the American land is open to a surprising range of contradictory symbolic interpretations. In *The Machine in the Garden,* Leo Marx notes, "A most striking fact about the New World was its baffling hospitality to radically opposed interpretations. If America seemed to promise everything that men always had wanted, it also threatened to obliterate much of what they had already achieved." Puritans viewed America as both a promised land and a howling wilderness, and many American writers since have considered the land with mixed feelings. For Washington Irving, nature represents both a sanctuary and a vaguely threatening place of disorientation, like the Kaatskills in "Rip Van Winkle"; for Thoreau, nature is spirit and beauty but also a setting for brutal instincts (his impulse in *Walden* to eat a woodchuck raw, for example). Such contradictory attitudes are amplified where the American West is concerned. In *Virgin Land,* Henry Nash Smith has shown that the West has been mythologized either as a garden or as the Great American Desert—myths that have polarized and distorted our views.⁴

Twain's initial portrayals of the West attempt to control or successfully negotiate such bifurcations. In an 1861 letter written to his mother and published in the *Keokuk Gate City,* Samuel Clemens has already begun to assume the basic literary personality of Mark Twain (though the name was not formally adopted until January 1863); and "Mark Twain" shows mixed feelings about the odor of sagebrush: "When crushed, sage-brush emits an odor which isn't exactly magnolia, and equally isn't polecat, but a sort of compromise between the two." Using humor as his mediator, Twain often molds his descriptions of the West so as to achieve a flexible stance that is not dominated by one fixed or extreme perspective. Indeed, Twain tends to accommodate a variety of viewpoints simultaneously. In this same letter he decries the West's aridity but praises its grand mountains; he frames this droll tribute to the West:

> I am *delighted* with it. It is the dustiest country on the face of the earth—but I rather like dust. And the days are very hot—but you know I am fond of hot days.—And the nights are cold—but one always sleeps well under blankets. And it never rains here—but I despise a country where rain and mud are fashionable. And there are no mosquitoes here—but then I can get along without them. And there are scorpions here—and tarantulas or spiders, as big as a mouse—but I am passionately fond of spiders. . . . I never liked any country so well before.⁵

Later, in a letter published in the *Virginia City Daily Territorial Enterprise,* Twain replies to a Missourian's letter requesting information about Nevada Territory (both the Missourian and his letter were probably invented by Twain): "On our ranches here, anything can be raised that can be produced on the fertile fields of Missouri. But ranches are very scattering—as scattering, perhaps, as lawyers in heaven."⁶ Correspondingly, Twain controls his "scattering" and incongruous depictions of the arid West; his humor moves lightly from one viewpoint to the next, effortlessly summoning comic similes. Twain implies that he won't be dominated by the West; his humor renders the West malleable to his diverse comic impulses.

For Twain, the frontier is an open land ready to be filled with the shapes of his own imagination, a land that can be either romantically glorified or undercut with relentless realism. Combining great mineral wealth and barrenness, Nevada Territory is particularly calculated to provoke his romanticism and his realism. While writing enthusiastically about Nevada's mines and reveling in statistics about ore production, Twain is also vaguely distrustful of the promise of Nevada Territory.[7] These mixed attitudes are epitomized in his October 1862 *Enterprise* article "The Spanish Mine." One of the richest on the Comstock Lode, the mine is described by Twain with wonder, humor, and anxiety. He praises the construction of the mine, its organization and management, and the richness of its specimens; he delights in the adventure of a visit, during which he descended several hundred feet into the mine, and uses sundry humorous touches and quaint figures of speech to enliven the account. Simultaneously, however, he expresses unease and disorientation: "A confused sense of being buried alive, and a vague consciousness of stony dampness, and huge timbers, and tortuous caverns, and bottomless holes with endless ropes hanging down them, and narrow ladders climbing in a short twilight through the colossal lattice work and suddenly perishing in midnight, and workmen poking about in the gloom with twinkling candles—is all, or nearly all that remains to us of our experience in the Spanish mine."[8] The threat of entombment is acute, and though Twain tries to laugh it off with humorous references to "the infernal regions" and "the confines of purgatory," he appears unsettled, for the mines of Nevada Territory do seem to have something hellish about them and the miners at times seem demonic. Twain may joke that the lesson of mine construction, if applied aboveground, would lead one to build the third story of a house first and proceed downward; but this article, as in many of his western writings, reveals a topsy-turvy world that sometimes his humor can control only partially. The West and the Sandwich Islands present spectacle and contradiction: Twain is bewildered by earthquakes and vagrant houses in San Francisco, bewitched by equatorial calms while en route to the Sandwich Islands, and awed by the fiery magnificence and terror of the island volcano Kilauea, which, as "the idea of eternity made tangible," impresses him much as the Sphinx does in *The Innocents Abroad.* Protean, fragmented, often without a stable pattern, the Mark Twain of these early writings is frequently shaped by disorienting encounters with the land itself. As Stephen Fender notes, the "jumbled" style of Twain's early western writings owes something to the "unresolved contrasts" of the West.[9]

Similarly, Twain confronts sharp cultural dichotomies between West and East. The East is settled, secure, and ruled by law and reason; the West is unsettled, dangerous, and ruled by force and fear. The East is predicated upon what is known; the West is predicated upon what is unknown, leaving vast space for rumors, exaggerations, and lies. Moreover, what William Dean Howells has remarked of the Middle West is even more true of the Far West: "Anyone who has really known the West (and really to know it one must have lived it) is aware of the profoundly serious, the almost tragical strain which is the fundamental tone in the movement of such music as it has."[10] The "tragical strain" of the West makes it hard at times for Twain to reshape the West, to transform it with his humor. Nevertheless, the strangeness, inchoateness, and contradictions of the West let Twain present comic ironies and adventures.

Twain presents the West as a place of deception and misinformation. Much of Nevada Territory's mining speculation runs on fantasy; the inflated mining stocks lead to exaggeration and invention in everyday conversation.[11] Montaigne's rule that one should not speak about that which one does not know becomes inverted in the West. As Twain explains in an 1864 piece for the *San Francisco Morning Call,* "In Washoe, if a man don't know anything, he will at least go on and tell you what he don't know, so that you can publish it in case you do not stumble upon something of more vital interest to the community, in the course of the day." Twain indicates that the main ore produced in the West is fantasy—simultaneously a dream and a nightmare for the humorist/journalist. Rumors abound. In an 1864 letter to the *Enterprise,* Twain notes: "There was a report about town, last night, that Charles Strong . . . had been shot and very effectually killed. I asked him about it at church this morning. He said there was no truth in the rumor. And speaking of the church, I am at this moment suffering with an itching to do up the fashions there, but I expect it might not be an altogether safe speculation."[12] Frequently Twain converts rumor into humor, and then turns the whole issue aside into a subject of his own choosing, into a "reality" that he controls. Here, the word *church,* with its customary connotations of truth and seriousness, ironically serves as a bridge to the topic of church fashions, where Twain plays on the word *speculation*. Twain hints that rumors, pretense, and speculation are everywhere. Indeed, Twain himself is given to "speculations" of all sorts, and he puts such speculations to both humorous and serious uses. By questioning and undercutting the "truth" of the West, he maintains the truth of his persona, the power of his narrative voice. In a world of illusions, he becomes what is real—his humorous presence is what reassures us.

At the same time, Twain indicates just how unsettled a world it is that has no bedrock of truth underlying it. In the following example, taken from the same piece, his tone is humorous yet mildly uneasy:

> And a general row ensued, in the course of which nine pistol shots were fired, one of which broke Millenovich's arm, and another entered his side, inflicting an ugly and probably fatal wound. I get this meagre and unsatisfactory statement from an eye-witness, who says "they made it so warm for him in there that he don't rightly know much about it." I entertain a similar opinion myself. Another witness tells me several outsiders were wounded by chance shots, but I have been unable to stumble upon any such.

In the violent and unreliable West, journalistic standards are different from those in the East; the West presented in Twain's writings has a freer, more volatile notion of "evidence" and "fact" than has the East. In the West, "truth" is not a fixed or a closed system—it is fluid, changing. The "looser" or more "open" western standards allow more play for Twain, but they also challenge his stability.

In this new world, Twain often presents the theme of initiation—a theme that runs, in one form or another, through many later writings. He sets up a division between tenderfoot and old-timer, naïve romantic and sophisticated cynic. Franklin R. Rogers argues that this pattern informs Clemens's early letters to his mother and the *Gate City,* in which he casts his mother as the ignorant romantic asking questions about the West, and himself as the worldly-wise realist answering her. In such letters Samuel Clemens has already begun to be Mark Twain. According to Rogers, this romantic-realist pattern is also used by Twain in *Roughing It,* in which he presents himself as both tenderfoot and old-timer.[13] Although the Mark Twain of

Roughing It is more complex than Rogers indicates, the division between uninitiated and initiated does affect the way in which Twain presents himself. Indeed, this division figured in the literary consciousness of Samuel Clemens from early on. One of his first published pieces, "The Dandy Frightening the Squatter" (written when Clemens was only sixteen), pits an eastern dandy, boastful but unacquainted with the ways of the Middle West, against a laconic Mississippi Valley squatter, with lamentable results for the dandy.

The contrast between West and East is also portrayed by Twain as primitivism versus sophistication, vigor versus sedateness, power fantasies versus conventional limitations. In *Roughing It,* Twain dramatizes this conflict by pitting a coyote against a town-dog; in his early writings for various western newspapers, principally the *Enterprise,* he often symbolizes the West through vulgar, uninhibited characters, usually based on actual persons whom Twain has "touched up" for the occasion. In many *Enterprise* writings Twain's symbol of the West is The Unreliable, who is based on rival *Union* reporter Clement T. Rice and is a prototype for the barbaric Mr. Brown. In a February 1863 *Enterprise* piece entitled "The Unreliable," Twain uses the title character as an epitome of the impoverished, uncultivated West:

> This poor miserable outcast crowded himself into the Firemen's Ball, night before last, and glared upon the happy scene with his evil eye for a few minutes. He had his coat buttoned up to his chin, which is the way he always does when he has no shirt on. As soon as the managers found out he was there, they put him out, of course. They had better have allowed him to stay, though, for he walked straight across the street, with all his vicious soul aroused, and climbed in at the back window of the supper room and gobbled up the last crumb of the repast provided for the guests, before he was discovered. This accounts for the scarcity of provisions at the Firemen's supper that night. Then he went home and wrote a particular description of our ball costume, with his usual meanness, as if such information could be of any consequence to the public. He never vouchsafed a single compliment to our dress, either, after all the care and taste we had bestowed upon it. We despise that man.[14]

The article's tone and style typify Twain's early western writings, and its subject and approach reflect Twain's mixed attitudes toward the West. On one hand, Twain has fun with his caricature of Rice; such humorous feuding between newspaper reporters was common in the Old West. On the other hand, Twain indicates repressed admiration for the marvelously uninhibited character of The Unreliable. At the end of the piece, Twain plays the part of eastern dandy, annoyed because The Unreliable "never vouchsafed a single compliment to our dress." At this moment, The Unreliable (and the vulgar but straightforward West) suddenly seems superior to the gentlemanly (and pretentious) Twain satirizing him. When Twain begins to use Mr. Brown, such complexities of tone reflect Twain's ambivalent feelings about the West, about primal vulgarity, about the conflict between realism and literary imagination, and about his persona and the uses of humor.

What is perhaps most striking in Twain's presentation of characters such as The Unreliable is his emphasis upon a childlike lack of restraint, a child's unsocialized and uninhibited ego that can veer either toward unreflective barbarism or toward sheer exuberance, a refreshing directness that manufactures fun. Twain shows that westerners are often childlike: they are blunt, emotional, given to violence and fantasy, and subject to many illusions. Like children, westerners inhabit a world simultaneously playful and nightmarish. The miners, gamblers, and desperadoes in Nevada Territory, similar to the half-civilized former cannibals Twain later describes in the Sandwich Islands, represent to him humanity uncovered, in its childhood stage. Like Melville, who had similar thoughts about the Typees and rough whalers, Twain speculates on what human nature is *really* like, for better or for worse, when stripped of its veneer of social forms, ideas, and customs. The writer whom most readers remember for his "celebration" of childhood shows even in these early writings an awareness of how "childish" human nature is—and how complex and ambiguous that childishness may be.

In one of his first pieces to gain national recognition, the February 1864 article "Those Blasted Children," Twain presents a hilarious picture of himself being annoyed by the rapscallion children of prominent westerners at San Francisco's Lick House.[15] In their quarrels, boasts, and games, the children are seen as miniature versions of their famous parents. Twain is besieged by these tiny tormentors, one of whom gleefully says, "Hi Johnny! look through the keyhole! here's that feller with a long nose, writing again—less [*sic*] stir him up!" Twain's relationship to these children resembles his relationship to The Unreliable or, later, to Mr. Brown: he is superior to them and mocks them with ironic humor, yet he is also a helpless victim before their vitality and irreverence. He laments, "Here come those young savages again—those noisy and inevitable children. God be with them!—or they with him, rather, if it be not asking too much." At times his pose toward children anticipates W. C. Fields's: a mixture of bewilderment, hostility, and fascination. Thus, Twain gives advice about curing childhood disorders: "In cases where an infant stammers, remove the under-jaw." And he concludes with this mock hymn to his own childhood: "O infancy! thou art beautiful, thou art charming, thou art lovely to contemplate! But thoughts like these recall sad memories of the past, of the halcyon days of my childhood, when I was a sweet, prattling innocent, the pet of a dear home-circle, and the pride of the village." The stilted, sugared prose makes the irony transparent, even for those who don't know that the boy Samuel Clemens was anything but a "sweet, prattling innocent." Twain's attitude toward children—and the childlike West—remains ambiguous. Disliking the unconscious cruelty embedded in much childlike behavior, Twain is nevertheless fascinated by the forthrightness of childlike characters.

His mixed attitudes toward children and childlike adults help shape his evolving attitude toward the world. He begins to blend a childlike, pleasure-loving side with an adult, critical side; he begins to develop humor that is simultaneously innocent and mature, direct and sophisticated. Such blending requires a fluid persona, not a static one given to artificial distinctions. As he evolves, Twain presents a childlike freshness and irreverence while considering ever more important philosophical and social issues.

The West thus poses for Twain various incongruities, ironies, and illusions: it is a vast and bewildering natural environment; it fosters a culture keenly different from that of the East; and it induces a childishness productive of both play and cruelty. Developing into a persona who can put such contradictions to his own comic uses, Twain often retaliates against the West; indeed, at times Twain seems at war with the world generally, with humor as his weapon. He fights illusion with illusion, chaos with chaos, primitivism with primitivism. Twain responds this way in part because of the influence of Southwestern humor. Humorists such as A. B. Longstreet, Johnson Hooper, T. B. Thorpe, and George Washington Harris, prominent from the 1830s to the 1850s, emphasized rustic primitives, hoaxes and pranks, violence, tall tales, superabundant energy, quaint or humorous dialect, and vulgarity.[16] Many of Twain's western characters resemble those depicted by Southwestern humorists; The Unreliable and Mr. Brown count Longstreet's Ned Brace, Hooper's Simon Suggs, Thorpe's Jim Doggett, and Harris's Sut Lovingood among their literary ancestors. Many Southwestern humorists were professional men originally from the Atlantic Coast or the North who felt bewildered by the Old Southwest, much as Twain did by the West. Their works use humor and condescension to describe native southwestern types; the authors preserve their sense of superiority while safely indulging in the zest and fun of the Old Southwest—much as Twain does in his western writings. Southwestern writers emphasize a humorous persona who can rise superior to primitive surroundings while yet enjoying those surroundings, and they are often fascinated by confidence men. The confidence game becomes a means of transforming and overcoming a troublesome reality—an idea also notable in Twain.

Twain's reliance upon Southwestern humorists, plus his exposure to the West, makes his writing characteristic of frontier humor in many ways. Bernard DeVoto, who has done the best job of detailing the frontier influence on Twain, claims that "all his life he was a story-teller, in the manner and idiom of the frontier." According to DeVoto, Twain's vision and style are those of the frontier: "The Western manner formed: cool, detached, unimpressible. Perhaps a theory would find an analogy in desert air which dissipates half lights and presents the true outline of objects undistorted."[17] A cool detachment does mark many of Twain's western writings, just as in those of the Southwestern humorists; in this attitude are the seeds of the transcendent detachment that characterizes Twain's late writings. Yet DeVoto, despite his knowledge of the West, may have forgotten that western air often does *not* show "the true outline of objects undistorted." Mirages shimmer in the desert; mountains appear deceptively near; mesas seemingly float in the dusk. The western manner is often not so clear or detached, and Twain's portrayal of the West is often shifting, ambiguous, and complex. In fact, so various are his literary efforts, humor, and poses that it sometimes appears that Twain has adopted the philosophy of Hooper's arch confidence man, Simon Suggs: "It is good to be shifty in a new country." A confidence man rises superior to his circumstances through variety, play, and poses; the danger lies in a loss of integrity, a loss of an integral self, and the risk of exposure and suffering.

In other ways Twain uses frontier humor to present himself as transcendent—or at least resilient. Twain engages in frontier forms of exaggeration, emphasizing physical discomfort or even death that can nonetheless be stoically faced. In his August 23, 1863, *Enterprise* letter from Steamboat Springs, he describes a frontier cure-all known as "wake-up-Jake": "If a man was low-spirited; if his appetite failed him; . . . if he were bilious; or in love; or in any other kind of trouble; or if he doubted the fidelity of his friends or the efficacy of his religion, there was always some one at his elbow to whisper, 'Take a "wake-up," my boy.'" Twain follows the advice, with surprising results:

> I swallowed the nauseous mess, and that one meal sufficed me for the space of forty-eight hours. And during all that time, I could not have enjoyed a viler taste in my mouth if I had swallowed a slaughter-house. I lay down with all my clothes on, and with an utter indifference to my fate here or hereafter, and slept like a statue from six o'clock until noon. I got up, then, the sickest man that ever yearned to vomit and couldn't. All the dead and decaying matter in nature seemed buried in my stomach, and I "heaved, and retched, and heaved again," but I could not compass a resurrection—my dead would not come forth. Finally, after rumbling, and growling, and producing agony and chaos within me for many hours, the dreadful dose began its work, and for the space of twelve hours it vomited me, and purged me, and likewise caused me to bleed at the nose.[18]

Twain pokes fun at the notion that a "tonic" can improve one's basic self; fundamental problems of body and soul are impervious to such remedies. Furthermore, the bitter yet comic incongruity here is that the "cure-all" is worse than the disorder, just as the supposed cure-all of western mineral wealth often led only to greater impoverishment. The West itself often makes Twain ill in all sorts of grotesque and ironic ways. Yet Twain survives—even "purges"—after a fashion.

Physical and mental suffering is frequent in Twain's writing, as it is in frontier writing generally.[19] Humorists recognized the harshness and incongruities of frontier life and tried to allay pain by converting it into humorous nonsense, as though one might banish the beast by laughing at it. Pain was so much the "raw material" of the frontier that it was what the humorist had to work with: one had to find a way to manufacture fun out of pain or not manufacture fun at all. Like many frontier humorists, Twain stresses an exuberant endurance necessary to frontier life—comic stoicism in the face of extreme suffering. In his 1863 piece "How to Cure a Cold," he details his tribulations in following home remedies; his account of his tortures anticipates his anecdotes in *The Innocents Abroad* about suffering at the hands of French barbers and Turkish masseurs. Or consider his accounts of his unpleasant experiences with horses, whether it be Oahu in the Sandwich Islands letters, Jericho in *The Innocents Abroad,* or the Mexican Plug in *Roughing It.* Suffering is not confined to the West. Repeatedly Twain shows the world, like his horses, to be a painful ordeal difficult to control; but he converts travail into comic capital, thereby giving himself a measure of invincibility.

In such ways Twain begins to confront not just frontier trials but also dilemmas inherent in life itself—existential problems that render life a frontier existence of sorts. For instance, in the "wake-up-Jake" passages, his description of love as another "kind of trouble" and of doubting "the fidelity of his friends or the efficacy of his religion" as a medical problem is quaint and funny; but Twain also prompts us to reflect upon some absurdities inherent in romantic love, friendship, and religion. After all, being in love sometimes does lead to sleeplessness and indigestion; though "wake-up-Jake" may not be the answer, some remedy is needed for this occasionally sorry human condition! Already Twain is able to inspire thought through a light touch—an ability he refines in later writings. Such humor makes him seem assured and wise even when beset by suffering and humiliation.

Similarly, his hoaxes, though following a well-established frontier tradition, at times move beyond pranks to suggest a vision of the world. Granted, on one level Twain's hoaxes represent mere bravado—a retaliation in kind against a West that constantly dupes him with its deceptive distances, freakish weather, deceitful people, and false promises of riches. Twain enjoys beating the West at its own tricks. Furthermore, Twain enjoys duping his readers as a way to regain control or mastery. Frequently he has specific targets in mind in his hoaxes. For instance, in "Petrified Man" (1862) he lampoons Justice of the Peace G. T. Sewall and the newspaper fad of reporting alleged petrifactions; in "A Bloody Massacre near Carson" (1863) he pokes fun at the owner of the Magnolia saloon, the Spring Valley Water Company of San Francisco, and newspapers that tout California stocks over Nevada stocks.

Twain's hoaxes, though, transcend particular targets to suggest something illusory in life itself, an instability or ambiguity in the way we perceive and learn about the world. Considering the "Petrified Man" hoax, Fender distinguishes between a "proper" hoax such as this one, which he considers "self-falsifying" because it has internal clues that tell a perceptive reader without any privileged knowledge it *is* a hoax, and a hoax such as "A Bloody Massacre near Carson," which he considers an "improper" hoax because supposedly only a local reader knowledgeable about local geography and people could see through it.[20] Such distinctions, however, break down when applied to Twain's hoaxes. Twain implies there are no sure standards of knowledge by which to determine what is false (or "self-falsifying") and what is true. To be sure, in the "Petrified Man" hoax, Twain describes the facial expression and hand position of the alleged petrified man in such a way that alert readers realize they are being mocked (the petrified man is thumbing his nose); but most of the piece is written in such a flat, reportorial style that even careful readers are puzzled, not knowing how to reconcile absurdity with a deadpan tone. In an article written eight years later for his *New York Galaxy* "Memoranda" column, Twain expresses the dilemma well: "From beginning to end the 'Petrified Man' squib was a string of roaring absurdities, albeit they were told with an unfair pretence of truth that even imposed upon me to some extent, and I was in some danger of believing in my own fraud." And, showing just how difficult truth is to come by, Twain turns *this* piece, purportedly explanatory, into a hoax in its own right: he invents details that were never in the original hoax and pretends that newspapers everywhere ran his original hoax as though it were genuine news.[21] With this follow-up article, as with the original, the reader is left cemented as fast to

Twain's ongoing hoax as the petrified man is to the rock. The reader cannot blast himself free to know what the truth is.

The hoax is even more complex in "A Bloody Massacre near Carson." Twain attributes the tale to Abram Curry, a longtime, reliable Washoe resident; Twain introduces Curry in *Roughing It* as the man who enlightened him as to what a Mexican Plug is. The hoax is thus given an air of authority. Moreover, bloody outrages were not unknown in Nevada Territory. Citing William C. Miller, Edgar M. Branch and Robert H. Hirst point out that Twain based his article on actual ax murders perpetrated by William Cornwell at Reese River the preceding year.[22] But as Twain explains in the same *Galaxy* piece, he provided clues to alert readers to the hoax: "The murderer was perfectly well known to every creature in the land as a *bachelor,* and consequently he could not murder his wife and nine children; he murdered them 'in his splendid dressed-stone mansion just in the edge of the great pine forest between Empire City and Dutch Nick's' when even the very pickled oysters that came on our tables knew that there was not a 'dressed-stone mansion' in all Nevada Territory." Twain adds that although his hoax had claimed there was a vast pine woods between Empire City and Dutch Nick's, there weren't any trees in the entire area; furthermore, it was well known that Empire City and Dutch Nick's were the *same* place. Finally, he notes the inclusion of a clue that should have revealed the hoax to even the most obtuse reader: "On top of all these absurdities I state that this diabolical murderer, after inflicting a wound upon himself that the reader ought to have seen would have killed an elephant in the twinkling of an eye, jumped on his horse and rode *four miles,* waving his wife's reeking scalp in the air, and thus performing entered Carson City with tremendous eclat, and dropped dead in front of the chief saloon, the envy and admiration of all beholders."[23] Twain plays games with this explanation, just as he did with his explanation of the "Petrified Man" hoax. His original hoax asserts that the murderer, Hopkins, lived in an "old log house," not in a "dressed-stone mansion" as Twain says in the *Galaxy* piece (Twain apparently manufactures a "quotation"), and thus the hoax lacks one of the clues Twain claims it has. Moreover, as Fender observes, some of the geographic and personal clues (place-names, the pine forest, Hopkins being a bachelor) would have been known only to local residents. Nonetheless, Twain might declare the hoax "self-falsifying" even by Fender's standards since his last point stands: it is patently absurd that a man could cut his own throat and then gallop about on his horse. Yet readers *were* duped. Twain presents a case he observed personally—or claims he did—in a Virginia City restaurant the morning his article first appeared. He says that "two stalwart innocents," whose "vegetable dandruff" revealed them to be hay truckers just in from the Truckee River, were dining nearby and that the one facing Twain was obviously reading Twain's "pleasant financial satire":

> From the way he was excitedly mumbling, I saw that the heedless son of a hay-mow was skipping with all his might, in order to get to the bloody details as quickly as possible; and so he was missing the guide-boards I had set up to warn him that the whole thing was a fraud. Presently his eyes spread wide open, just as his jaws swung asunder to take in a potato approaching it on a fork; the potato halted, the face lit up redly, and the whole man was on fire with excitement. Then he broke into a disjointed checking-off of the particulars—his potato cooling in mid-air meantime, and his mouth making a reach for it occasionally, but always bringing up suddenly against a new and still more direful performance of my hero. At last he looked his stunned and rigid comrade impressively in the face, and said, with an expression of concentrated awe:
> "Jim, he b'iled his baby, and he took the old 'oman's skelp. Cuss'd if *I* want any breakfast!"
> And he laid his lingering potato reverently down, and he and his friend departed from the restaurant empty but satisfied.[24]

Whether Twain is reporting or inventing this scene, his anecdote suggests why so many readers were duped: they wanted to be duped, no matter how much they howled about it later (and a howl did go up, from Nevada Territory to the Pacific Coast, with deceived newspaper editors leading the chorus). Just as they were anxious to accept myths about the West's mineral wealth, readers were so eager for sensational news that they duped themselves. Indeed, they tended to exaggerate horrors, as in the hay trucker declaring that Hopkins "b'iled his baby" when, "in fact," Hopkins brained the infant with a club. Even if Twain manufactured this anecdote about the hay trucker, what he indicates about human nature is reliable enough— the desire for myth, legend, and lie, to be "empty but satisfied."

The West was a place of extremes, as was much of western humor, according to Fender.[25] The reason was not just the West's climate and geography; human nature and fancy, left to run riot in a world devoid of cultural norms and secure standards of knowledge, often inclined toward sensationalism, toward what was new, melodramatic, or horrific. We should not condescend to the hay trucker too much, for the only difference between him and us, in our sensationalized age, is that most of us would have finished our meal—we would have "supped full with horrors."

"A Bloody Massacre near Carson," like the "Petrified Man" hoax, is effective also because it so adroitly presents the sensational as fact. Twain gives the ages of several murdered children, the disposition of their bodies, and the statements of two surviving children. Even the satiric ending, which explains that Hopkins went mad because he had sold all his Nevada mining stock for worthless California stock, seems to be logical speculation as to motive. Indeed, one senses here what Twain confessed about the "Petrified Man" hoax: the subtle process by which, in the very act of writing a hoax, the writer becomes engaged in the illusion he has created until, though he does not actually come to believe in the hoax himself, he becomes committed to it. Some of Twain's later writings present dreamers who become enmeshed in their own dreams—dreamers who dream themselves, as hoaxers may hoax themselves. What we may note about "A Bloody Massacre near Carson" is that both the vividness of the hoax and its authoritative, reportorial tone go beyond the demands of mere satire (Twain's avowed intention). What is at work here goes deeper, to the heart of Twain's developing control of his material. In part it is the fun of fantasy and creation, plus the sense of mastery invoked by fooling one's readers. But what is also suggested is a sophisticated relationship between Twain and his world, whereby Twain tries to make that world malleable through narrative.

So much of Twain's writing naturally and casually depends on exaggeration, distortion, and illusion that often we hardly notice these techniques. It isn't true, for example, that sagebrush smells like both magnolia and polecat, yet we accept this description. Our implicit consent to the imagination's ability to transform the world lets Twain manufacture comic exaggerations at will. By creating illusions and emphasizing the ambiguity of experience, Twain can dissolve the world into something he can shape and control. The danger is that sometimes illusions can trap the writer in a "fun house" of his own making, as in some of Twain's later narratives; if the illusions turn dark and frightening, the illusionist may not have a secure reality to retreat to. But in these early writings Twain's creation of illusions lets him engage in humorous play. Even in the more extreme and potentially threatening form of the hoax, even when Twain confesses to almost duping himself, he still implies that it's all justified by gains in freedom and humor—the tone of such pieces is almost always buoyant. Twain is liberated, not diminished or endangered, by his transformations of the world.

Twain also puts illusion-making to more speculative uses. After all, to some extent literature by nature is a hoax and the writer a confidence man. Branch notes in *The Literary Apprenticeship of Mark Twain,* "Before he was done, Mark Twain must have learned something about that skill in writing that makes all literature, viewed as an imitation of actuality, a kind of hoax—but a hoax whose seriousness cannot be in doubt." A writer builds illusory worlds that he tries to dupe the reader into regarding as "real." Furthermore, a humorist such as Twain who wants to express (often covertly) serious ideas may frequently engage in hoaxes about his intentions. William Kaufman observes, "The primary requisite of [Twain's] art as comedian lay in convincing his audience that his words were in jest in spite of the underlying awareness that the opposite was true; this is the comedian's confidence-game, his masquerade."[26] Twain often hoaxes his readers—and perhaps even himself—as to what his "real" motives are. By volatilizing world and experience, by unsettling concepts and conventions, Twain can offer both comic and serious themes, often simultaneously.

Twain seems modern in his fascination with hoaxes, illusions, and exaggerations. We who have grown accustomed to "the big lie," whether it be in politics, economics, or war, find that Twain's indulgence in hoaxes mirrors our own sense of a deceptive world. In *The Put-on: Modern Fooling and Modern Mistrust,* Jacob Brackman defines the "put-on artist" as one who has "a pervasive style of relating to others that perpetually casts what he says into doubt. The put-on is an *open-end* form. That is to say, it is rarely climaxed by having the 'truth' set straight—when a truth, indeed, exists." Brackman adds that there are no simple rules for understanding what the put-on artist means; for instance, we can't assume that he is being ironical and means precisely the opposite of what he says. "The put-on, inherently, *cannot* be understood." Although Brackman does not discuss Twain, we may regard Twain as a put-on artist. Twain's hoaxes do not reduce to set meanings; many of his other writings, though not explicitly hoaxes, have similar ambiguities. Brackman's justification for the put-on might also be Twain's defense of his indulgence in hoax: "It may be that the put-on offers the only remaining possibility for aesthetic or philosophical synthesis in a world that has become staggeringly confused and grotesque. It may be that when reality becomes too complex to master, the best we can do is adopt an attitude toward it." In other words, it may be that the world intrinsically resists interpretation and rational explanation, in which case the hoax mirrors a complex and relativistic world, a world where there may be no final objectivity or absolute truth. In *Mark Twain's Humor: The Image of a World,* Pascal Covici Jr. argues that Twain's hoaxes are of the "incompleted-ending variety"; Covici adds that "it is the nature of a hoax to displace suddenly one set of perceptions by another."[27] But Covici may be assuming a stable world in his notion that hoaxes strip away pretense and offer "sudden revelation," whereas Brackman's notion of an inherently put-on world is more applicable to Twain's sense of the world and his hoaxes.

In these early hoaxes Twain begins a pattern that persists through his later writings. He indicates that the world is an intricate, shifting, and relativistic place; he begins to develop a flexible response to that world. Later, Twain experiments with the idea that even the self may be a hoax; the belief that the "I" is integral, a unit, may be an illusion. Twain becomes increasingly multiplistic, exhibiting a sophisticated play of attitudes; his humor shows that both world and self are *processes,* changing and relativistic, not static entities. Just as the put-on suggests there is no final form or "truth" to the world, Twain's writing suggests there is no final form to the self, to consciousness. Instead, "truth" consists of freedom, humor, and variety of vision. Twain evolves a frontier pragmatism in which truth and value are equated with his humor and resourcefulness.

Such relativism has its price. Even in an early hoax such as "A Bloody Massacre near Carson" Twain seems uneasy at times, as

though unsure how to define himself or his relationship to an illusory world. The world this hoax sets up is ghastly and violent: Hopkins murders his children and scalps his wife. Scholars have frequently pointed out the violence in Twain's narratives. Some of this
violence may be due to frontier traditions; some may be due to the
psychological makeup of Samuel Clemens.[28] Twain presents the ambiguity of experience both as an opportunity for play and as a threat
that undermines reason and identity. The violence in Twain's humor reflects the violence or, more accurately, the disorder in the
world, in his writings, and in himself as a literary (and hence created)
personality. His violent humor also suggests mixed attitudes about
the self as a participant in—and even as a promoter of—a chaotic
world. In short, Twain seems ambivalent about his role as hoaxer,
poser, and master illusionist. When, before the murders, poor Mrs.
Hopkins seeks help from others by describing her husband's fits of
madness, Twain says, "It was Mrs. Hopkins' misfortune to be given
to exaggeration, however, and but little attention was paid to what
she said." Twain depicts her as having a significant physical mark:
"The long red hair of the scalp he [Hopkins] bore marked it as that
of Mrs. Hopkins." Finally, Twain describes a peculiar mutilation: "her
right hand [was] almost severed from the wrist."[29] Again there may
be personal, psychological undertones here: when we recollect that
Samuel Clemens was given to exaggeration (especially as the writer
Mark Twain), that he also had reddish hair (a fact of which he was
particularly cognizant, as witnessed by his early piece "Oh, She Has
a Red Head!" in praise of redheads), and that he wrote with his right
hand, then his description of Mrs. Hopkins and her fate is suggestive,
to say the least. Like the little boy who cried wolf, Mrs. Hopkins cannot compel anyone to believe her when the time for fact and seriousness comes; as Mark Twain inventing fictions, including this whole
narrative about Mrs. Hopkins, Samuel Clemens may have feared a
similar fate.

Twain may not only be caught in his own hoax but also, like the
reader, not know what context to set it in. Recall that a significant
feature of both "Petrified Man" and "A Bloody Massacre near Carson"
is the way in which the sensational is mixed with the ordinary. One
reason we sometimes cannot be sure how to read Twain is that so
often he mixes fact and fancy, humor and atrocity, all the while play-

ing with frames of reference. Perhaps such mixtures reflect experience itself—life as fraught with confusion and punctuated randomly by horrific occurrences. At any rate, in pieces such as "A Bloody Massacre near Carson" Twain seems to militate against clear patterns or meanings.

Such incongruity or disruption marks many of Twain's early works. His use of burlesque and satire, his playing with illusions, fantasy, and language, and his experiments with humor as both exploration and explosion reveal issues akin to those in his hoaxes. For example, hoax and burlesque often blend: both "Petrified Man" and "A Bloody Massacre near Carson" mimic sensationalism. Moreover, his hoaxes suggest a basic disorder in existence, and his burlesques push this point further, suggesting, as Cox notes, that life is absurd.[30] Like his hoaxes, Twain's burlesques range widely. He burlesques popular romances in "Aurelia's Unfortunate Young Man," in which the fair Aurelia wonders how long she should keep loving her unfortunate young man as he continues to lose various parts of his anatomy; he burlesques newspaper reporting in "The Killing of Julius Caesar 'Localized,'" in which he imagines the way in which a "western-style" newspaper reporter would have written up Caesar's murder; he burlesques advice columns in "Answers to Correspondents," in which he offers a hodgepodge of absurd suggestions; and he burlesques condensed novels and wartime romances in "Lucretia Smith's Soldier," in which Lucretia tends a wounded soldier, swathed in bandages like a mummy, only to discover that he is not *her* soldier after all. In such pieces it is difficult to determine whether fun or satire predominates.

We've seen that Twain often blurs the line between humor and satire; when Twain is immersed in illusion-making and rendering himself as a fluid persona, he shows little regard for conventional distinctions. This point helps explain why scholars have offered such radically different interpretations of what Twain is doing in these early pieces. Cox and Branch declare that Twain's western writings stress fun, not satire; Benson and Bellamy maintain that Twain emerges as an important social satirist in his western writings.[31] Such differences in perspective are easy to understand if we consider a sample passage from a Twain burlesque, a mock fashion report entitled "The Lick House Ball":

Mrs. A. W. B. was arrayed in a sorrel organdy, trimmed with fustians and figaros, canzou fichus, so disposed as to give a splendid effect without disturbing the general harmony of the dress. The body of the robe was of zero velvet, goffered, with a square pelerine of solferino *poil de chevre* amidships. The fan used by Mrs. B. was of real palm-leaf and cost four thousand dollars—the handle alone cost six bits. Her head dress was composed of a graceful cataract of white chantilly lace, surmounted by a few artificial worms, and butterflies and things, and a tasteful tarantula done in jet. It is impossible to conceive of anything more enchanting than this toilet—or the lady who wore it, either, for that matter.[32]

Twain satirizes women's fashions and the way newspapers report them. Yet the passage erupts into such nonsense that absurdity may overwhelm satire. Moreover, the passage shifts so frequently in meaning, tone, and language that the reader may feel bewildered. Many of Twain's terms, while sounding absurd to a modern reader, are actually proper: *organdy, fichus, goffered,* and *pelerine,* for example. On the other hand, terms such as *figaros* and *canzou* are misused or even invented, while it is unlikely that the dignified Mrs. B. was clad in *poil de chevre* (goat hair) or would enjoy having her middle referred to as *amidships.* But then there are various terms that are "amidships" in meaning. *Sorrel,* for instance, might properly mean a light reddish color, or it might less properly mean a horse of this color, tying in with other animal and insect images in the passage. Or it might mean a plant with acid leaves and sour juice—strangely appropriate, given the tang of the passage. Similarly, *fustians* might mean cotton and flax fabrics, or it might mean passages of bombast—singularly apt for a paragraph of claptrap. In short, Twain plays with language, using words with multiple meanings so that the reader has no proper context for understanding.

In other fashion burlesques, Twain sometimes challenges our use of language even more openly, as in this passage from the "Pioneers' Ball": "Mrs. C. N. was superbly arrayed in white kid gloves. Her modest and engaging manner accorded well with the unpretending simplicity of her costume, and caused her to be regarded with absorbing interest by every one."[33] Twain implies that we often use language in ways that don't accord with reality or convey what we really mean; there is a fundamental absurdity to our everyday use of language, an absurdity that may be viewed either satirically or humorously, or both, depending on one's temperament. There is often a "gap" between word and world, a space wherein Twain may play.

Naturally, there is a temptation to look for some concrete structural principles behind Twain's early writings. Thus, in *Mark Twain's Burlesque Patterns,* Rogers argues that the writing of burlesques led Twain to develop "three major and distinctive structural devices," including the alternation of serious and humorous events.[34] Platform personality Mark Twain at times alternated serious and humorous anecdotes in his monologues; certainly some of that pattern emerges in his writing. Usually, though, Twain does not so much alternate the serious and the humorous as commingle them, again indicating why it is virtually impossible to delineate satire from humor in many Twain pieces. Twain's burlesques and hoaxes suggest that *all* representation may be, in some ways, mocking or illusory; the way consciousness filters experience may inevitably lead to the kind of distortion and nonsense found in his works. Often there may be no sure standards for marking off what is "serious" from what is "humorous." The world may be a messy, fluid place; certainly it is in Twain's writings.

Twain's protean humor, presenting a protean world, also begins to present—or create—a protean self. That is, Twain's variable humor not only presents a changeable and illusory world but also renders him a variable and manifold presence in his works. Humor and persona are interwoven: the more Twain depends on changeable humor for his expression, his very being as persona, the more changeable he becomes. Linked by humor, Twain and his world become mirror images of each other in their fluidity and relativism. As a persona, Twain is expressed through language, the medium we use to understand the world; much of his humor depends on showing how unstable language is. Twain becomes as fluid as the world his humor presents.

Questions of identity emerge. While "Aurelia's Unfortunate Young Man" burlesques popular romances, it also prompts speculation about what constitutes the self. At what point does the unfortunate young man, losing his bodily parts one by one, cease to be the man Aurelia originally loved? One might argue that a person is still the same being no matter how many limbs are lost, although troubling questions regarding the mind-body relationship might be raised. But what if memories, perceptions, and attitudes are also lost or changed? The predicament of the fair Aurelia might mockingly recall that of the fair Ophelia, who wonders how to regard Hamlet as he seemingly loses his mind and undergoes a significant personality change. Such issues seem to perplex an ever-changing Twain. In "Lucretia Smith's Soldier," a case of mistaken identity leads Lucretia to attend to the wrong soldier—an error suggesting just how easily "identity" may be misperceived. In "Answers to Correspondents" Twain leads a "discarded lover" (seeking redress because his beloved has married another) on a merry, legal, linguistic, and philosophical chase, before finally concluding, dizzily enough: "I think I could take up the argument where I left off, and by following it closely awhile, perhaps I could prove to your satisfaction, either that you never existed at all, or that you are dead now, and consequently don't need the faithless Edwitha—I think I could do that, if it would afford you any comfort."[35] On one level this piece is mere nonsense; on another level it foreshadows many of Twain's later writings, preoccupied with questions of what it means to be an "I," a self. Just as love cannot be formulated by law or reason, perhaps neither can consciousness.

Perhaps much of life cannot be formulated. As Constance Rourke notes, the frontier celebrated liars and tricksters, and we've seen that such confidence men often managed to overcome their circumstances.[36] They succeeded because they undermined artificial forms, challenging the formal expectations and beliefs of others. One reason the West—and America generally—has been fascinated by confidence men is that the West has been inherently a place of deception, mocking many of the set social forms and beliefs of the Old World and suggesting that a supposedly circumscribing reality can be transcended. We have seen how variously the democratic West celebrates anything that denies fixity and finality. Democracy implies social fluidity. Though democracy can represent high ideals, it also often contains an element of trickery and deception—one reason, perhaps, why we have counted so many trickster figures among our political leaders. In the West, amid tall tales, exuberance, and social fluidity, trickery thrived.

Twain uses his fantasies and exaggerations, just as he uses his hoaxes and burlesques, to mirror his sense that there is no fixity, no final "truth" or "reality," in most experience. As Cox puts it, "In a world of lies, the tall tale is the only true lie because it does not mask as the truth but moves the listener to ask what the truth is."[37] Twain suggests that "truth" is often something that is *created,* dependent on a particular perspective, constructed order, controlled game, or system of beliefs that may, in itself, be a marvelous illusion. Within limits, the individual may in effect create his own world; the wide-open, unformulated West allowed for many such worlds. There is, of course, the danger that these various worlds will degenerate into *nothing but* lies and disillusionment—a persistent threat in the West, with its wildcat mines and broken dreams. But if one is willing to change the notion of "truth" and accept an unstable reality, then freedom and personal mobility may be gained. In the Old World, the "truth" was that one was defined by the social class one was born into; in the New World, as Franklin observed, the "truth" was that one was what one did—a protean conception of social position and identity. Although it is doubtful whether Franklin ever envisaged the kind of personal fluidity Twain projects, the American conception of individualism promulgated by Franklin and others helped lay the basis for Twain's ideas concerning persona, identity, and reality. (It is worth remembering that Franklin was at times a trickster himself, leaving his lamp burning while he slept so that others would think he was studying late into the night.) In his presentation of the West, Twain simply takes this imaginative and pragmatic individualism further.

As a western newspaperman in the early 1860s, Samuel Clemens found himself in a world in which reporters, those appointed conveyers of facts, were expected to engage in exaggeration to match the fantasies of their freewheeling readers. Henry Nash Smith and Frederick Anderson note that Nevada journalism was given to humor and fantasy. Indeed, many people in Nevada Territory tended to use language to shape reality—a process that extended even to the territorial legislature, on many of whose sessions Clemens reported. For instance, William Stewart, legislator and eventually senator from Nevada, opposed a bill to tax undeveloped mining property by "construing" the definition of "mine" so that a mine not yet profitable was not a mine at all. As Clemens once noted, "Bill Stewart is always construing something—eternally distorting facts and principles. . . .

He is a long-legged, bull-headed, whopper-jawed, constructionary monomaniac. Give him a chance to construe the sacred law, and there wouldn't be a damned soul in perdition in a month."[38] In an age when taxes are "revenue enhancements," we have become accustomed to such "construing"; for Samuel Clemens, however, such games may have proved both enlightening and threatening. Listening to Stewart, he perhaps had a foreboding of Will Rogers's famous quip: "I don't make jokes. I just watch the government and report the facts." But as Mark Twain, he quickly proved capable of such "construing" for his own comic purposes, as in *his* definition of a mine: "A hole in the ground with a fool at the end of it." In many Twain pieces, definitions are up for grabs; like Carroll's Humpty Dumpty, Twain insists that words mean what he wants them to mean. In the looking-glass worlds that Twain presents, "meaning" frequently varies.

There is a charm to Twain's linguistic play. Even his routine reporting frequently bursts into comic song, so to speak. As Branch declares, "Often the expression seems spontaneously original, like a reflex of sheer linguistic exuberance."[39] Even when writing about relatively staid San Francisco as a local reporter for the *Morning Call,* Twain sends up fireworks. He reports that a skyrocket went up, and his humor soars with it; when the rocket comes down, Twain is all ready for it:

Night before last, a stick six or seven feet long, attached to an exploded rocket of large size[,] came crashing down through the zinc roof of a tenement in Milton Place, Bush street, between Dupont and Kearny, passed through a cloth ceiling, and fetched up on the floor alongside of a gentleman's bed, with a smash like the disruption of a china shop. We have been told by a person with whom we are not acquainted, and of whose reliability we have now no opportunity of satisfying ourselves, as he has gone to his residence, which is situated on the San José road at some distance from the city, that when the rocket tore up the splinters around the bed, the gentleman got up. The person also said that he went out—adding after some deliberation, and with the air of a man who has made up his mind that what he is about to say can be substantiated if necessary, that "he went out quick." This person also said that after the gentleman went out quick, he ran—and then with a great show of disinterestedness, he ventured upon the conjecture that he was running yet. He hastened to modify this rash conjecture, however, by observing that he had no particular reason for suspecting that the gentleman was running yet—it was only a notion of his, and just flashed on him, like. He then hitched up his team, which he observed parenthetically that he wished they belonged to him, but they didn't, and immediately drove away in the direction of his country seat. The tenement is there yet, though, with the hole through the zinc roof. . . . The man who set it [the rocket] off, and hung on to it, and went up with it, has not come down yet. The people who live in Milton Place are expecting him, all the time. They have moved their families, and got out of the way, so as to give him a good show when he drops. They have said, but without insisting on it, that if it would be all the same to him, they would rather he would fall in the alley. . . . The Board of Supervisors will probably pass an ordinance directing that missiles of the dangerous nature of rockets shall henceforth be fired in the direction of the Bay, so as to guard against accidents to life and property.[40]

In his opening sentence, Twain carefully establishes the facts of his report: he tells when and where the accident occurred and even what type of roof (zinc) and ceiling (cloth) the skyrocket passed through. He drops some sensible advice in his last sentence, urging against any future such accident. But sandwiched between his matter-of-fact opening and closing is a "report" that he construes into nonsense, comic exaggeration, digression, and flights of fancy. Indeed, Twain presents a world that makes little sense and resists interpretation: What are we to make of the poker-faced wit of Twain's "informant"? Is this man really stealing a team of horses? Who set off the rocket and what actually happened to him? Do we live in a world where things just happen, just fall down upon us? Twain tells us that the hole in the zinc roof is there yet; anyone may go and make of it what he will. Twain indicates that the supposedly mundane world we take for granted can, with just a slightly different perspective, reveal depths of humorous absurdity. The surface of a fact may, at any moment, implode into comic chaos.

Such absurdity demands a versatile style. In "Mark Twain and the Myth of the West" Harold H. Kolb Jr. notes that Twain develops "a pyrotechnic style made up of exploding rhetorical flourishes, imploding understatements, juxtapositions sharpened at both ends, and a kaleidoscope of vernaculars."[41] Nowhere is this "pyrotechnic style" more evident than in the linguistic bursts Twain often sends up—his mixing of, and playing with, languages. Just as in his articles on women's fashions, Twain uses linguistic play to suggest life's confusions. It is another way of responding sportively to a multifaceted world and of developing himself as a variegated persona.

Writing about the San Francisco police courts for the *Morning Call,* Twain suggests he is witnessing the Tower of Babel anew: he describes people of every conceivable background, tongue, and dialect contradicting one another on every possible point. He notes, "It is a daily occurrence in the Police Court for men and women to mount the witness stand and swear to statements diametrically opposite."[42] Twain shows the diversity of human languages and perspectives; in many subsequent narratives he indicates that such diversity is a comic cacophony that may nevertheless at moments achieve a peculiar harmony. The art of humorous linguistic discord and idiomatic idiosyncrasies peaks in the Scotty Briggs anecdote in *Roughing It,* but even in his earlier writings Twain engages in sophisticated linguistic play.

Twain's emphasis on a linguistic kaleidoscope reflects a multifaceted world and self. Samuel Clemens's diverse occupations, experiences, and readings gave him various specialized vocabularies and viewpoints that, as Mark Twain, he tries to accommodate. In *The Art of Mark Twain,* William M. Gibson notes Twain's fondness for the specialized vocabularies of the river pilot, the printer, and the miner. Often Twain renders these different vocabularies as different worlds, each with its own set of beliefs, values, and views—worlds that he can enter and exit at will. As Jeffrey L. Duncan says, Twain's languages, especially when humorous, *become* experience: "Instead of conveying an original experience, his words constitute the original experience: the humor is inseparable, even theoretically, from its formulation, and the formulation exists, not for the sake of telling the empirical truth, but for the sake of the humor, the aesthetic idea."[43] In other words, Twain's work anticipates the modern idea that, to a large extent, language *is* thought and experience, that the words one uses shape the event described. More important, his use of language to construct "experience" or "truth" within a narrative is another way for him to shape his world, to make it controllable play.

Mixing vocabularies offers sportive and semantic possibilities. Twain mixes the languages of love and law in "Ye Sentimental Law Student," the terminologies of religion and mining in "The New Wildcat Religion," the vocabularies of whaling and everyday social conversation in "Mrs. Jollopson's 'Gam,'" and the expressions of marriage ceremonies and mining stock speculation in "Our Stock Remarks." The reader may feel as though he has multiple vision or is looking at the world through differently colored transparencies simultaneously. Because humor often depends on incongruity, such linguistic discords promote laughter; but Twain also uses them to unsettle the reader, strip away pretense, and suggest what a pluralistic world we live in. In "Our Stock Remarks" Twain presents the notes of an inebriated reporter who has confused a wedding with a market report:

> Owing to the fact that our stock reporter attended a wedding last evening, our report of transactions in that branch of robbery and speculation is not quite as complete and satisfactory as usual this morning. . . . Here are the notes: "Stocks brisk, and Ophir [a leading Comstock mine] has taken this woman for your wedded wife. Some few transactions have occurred in rings and lace veils, and at figures tall, graceful and charming. There was some inquiry late in the day for parties who would take them for better or for worse, but there were few offers. There seems to be some depression in this stock. We mentioned yesterday that our Father which art in heaven. Quotations of lost reference, and now I lay me down to sleep," & c., & c., &c.[44]

Twain distances himself from this muddled account by ascribing it to a colleague; furthermore, he reports this colleague as drunk and therefore liable to mix languages. Initially we may accept the piece as light humor, but then we have an afterthought: marriage *is* a "speculation," as risky as any mining speculation. Moreover, there is something "businesslike" in the marriage ceremony—it is a transaction, after all, no matter how one romanticizes it. Twain's first sentence makes it unclear whether "our report of transactions in that branch of robbery and speculation" refers to mining stocks or marriage ceremonies. We feel the ground cut from beneath us, much as when we read a Twain hoax or burlesque. The mixing of languages has made us question some illusions about marriage and left us wondering what perspective or context the sketch means to adopt.

What Twain develops most from such linguistic jouissance is multiple vision. As in his hoaxes and burlesques, Twain casts one thing in terms of another, playing with languages as he plays with perspectives. For example, in "The Great Prize Fight" he describes two prominent California political figures as prizefighters dismantling each other. Just as he does in "Our Stock Remarks," Twain opens a familiar subject in new ways, in this case prompting us to consider how political races sometimes degenerate into barbarism.

Experimenting with linguistic styles, Twain mixes tones and attitudes: "Since I have been in the city, the child of an indigent woman has lain four days unburied because of this quarrel between the police, the Mayor, and the county. However, the child was not dead, and so I suppose there wasn't really any occasion to bury it." Aggravated with his horse Oahu in the Sandwich Islands, he declares, "I was literally dripping with perspiration and profanity." In an *Enterprise* letter about going to the Logan Hotel on Lake Tahoe, he notes, "Thither I go to recuperate. I take with me a broken spirit, blighted hopes and a busted constitution. Also some gin."[45] Ordinarily, a reader is led by conventional linguistic and semantic expectations into often anticipating what a writer will say next, as though writer and reader implicitly agree on what the world is and consent to the same principles of thought. But such is not the case with Twain when he is at his playful best. Just as in his hoaxes, burlesques, and fantasies, Twain's linguistic games keep the reader guessing by shifting tones, perspectives, and contexts. The reader is led from the logical to the absurd, from the lofty to the vulgar (or vice versa), from one language or value system to another. Such linguistic light-footedness lets Twain wander where he chooses and not be tied to any one perspective. He shows that many of our ideas about the world and ourselves are rooted in associated contexts; stripping away such contexts allows for new, unsettling possibilities. Philological play lets him suggest what an intricate, messy, funny business life is, and how little we understand it—or ourselves—despite our pretensions. Yet Twain also suggests that life is subject to control, at least in part.

In these examples, as in most of Twain's best humor, there is a movement, an energy, that overrides everything, including conflicts, sordidness, and suffering. This restless energy makes the kaleidoscope of perspectives possible and holds forth the potential to reshape the world imaginatively. Even death may be recast. Indeed, Twain's ability to make death seem relatively nonthreatening may be one of his strongest appeals to us, as evidenced in this passage from "Early Rising, As Regards Excursions to the Cliff House":

> They entirely despaired of my recovery, at one time, and began to grieve for me as one whose days were numbered—whose fate was sealed—who was soon to pass away from them forever, and from the glad sunshine, and the birds, and the odorous flowers, and murmuring brooks, and whispering winds, and all the cheerful scenes of life, and go down into the dark and silent tomb—and they went forth sorrowing, and jumped a lot in the graveyard, and made up their minds to grin and bear it with that fortitude which is the true Christian's brightest ornament.[46]

Twain may be exaggerating the effects of a hangover, but the vitality pervading such writing suggests that he might indeed achieve psychological victory over almost any terror, including death. His playful use of poetic clichés suggests how stereotyped and artificial our customary views of life and death may be—and that a vigorous humor might let us transcend such views. Twain shows life to be a zestful, absurd affair—perhaps zestful *because* absurd. Celebrating the Chapman family, an aged western dramatic troupe accustomed to representing life in its many varieties, Twain presents life as a wonderful, ludicrous dance. He pays tribute to Mother Chapman, seventy-five years old and playing Mazeppa during a bitter winter in Montana Territory:

> The idea of the jolly, motherly old lady stripping to her shirt and riding a fiery untamed Montana jackass up flights of stairs and kicking up and cavorting around the stage on him with the quicksilver frozen in the thermometers and the audience taking brandy punches out of their pockets and biting them, same as people eat peanuts in civilized lands! Why, there is no end to the old woman's energy. She'll go through with Mazeppa with flying colors even if she has to do it with icicles a yard long hanging to her jackass's tail.[47]

Such energy, Twain suggests, is better than any philosophy, for it embodies the verve and creativity of life itself. The question is what to do with it.

When DeVoto and Gibson separately declare that Twain in his frontier writings already displays virtually all the stances and stylistic effects of his later writings, they are essentially correct.[48] His later narratives do become more sophisticated, addressing ever more complex issues of selfhood; but even in his early writings Twain presents a multiversant world and self. Like the Chapman family, Twain loves exuberance and drama, particularly self-dramatization. He ceaselessly exhibits his play of attitudes, his ability to respond to life in ever-new ways; he dramatizes himself as engaged in one comic adventure after another. For Twain the world is a fresh and wonderfully wacky place; he is free to call things the way he wants, free to make his own idiosyncratic associations of thought and perception. It is a world in which he is always at the center, his comic creative power naming that world to us. Given to such histrionics, then, Twain begins evolving into a persona capable of sustained self-dramatization. This emerging Mark Twain points toward the direction his humor and imagination will take in later narratives.

But problems remain. Studying the early Twain shows how much he sometimes takes his pen name to heart, for "doubleness" is a periodic theme; yet Twain's experiments with doubleness or an other-self schema are usually regressions and failures. These experiments are restrictive: the polarized emphasis is on conflict, not play, and strict dualities do not permit a mixing or shifting of viewpoints. It would be nice to say that all such lapses occur in Twain's earliest narratives but, alas, Twain, just as in his presentation of life itself, is messy. Although his increasing mastery of hoaxes, burlesques, fantasies, and linguistic play promotes flexibility, Twain sometimes still resorts to the relatively rigid structure of dualism. One of his most extended experiments in dualism, his use of Mr. Brown (with Brown as realist and Twain as romantic), occurs in his Sandwich Islands correspondence, *after* his Nevada and California journalism. Indeed, in various later writings Twain makes forays into dualities that are similarly confining.

There are several possible reasons for Twain's periodic presentation of doubleness. One, much discussed by scholars, is his tendency to express both romantic and realistic views of the world. Thus, Branch says that Twain's apprentice writings show "the intimate alliance of realist and romantic," a view I would qualify by saying the relationship is usually a war, not an alliance.[49] Rogers contends that Twain establishes a polarity in his early letters between a naïve, romantic inquirer and a sophisticated, cynical explicator of the West—a pattern Rogers believes is continued into *Roughing It* as a dualism between tenderfoot and old-timer. Furthermore, Twain's later fascination with twins (as in *Those Extraordinary Twins*) is foreshadowed in his habit of pairing himself with, or against, another—as, for instance, in his comic feuding with The Unreliable, whose brashness and vulgarity anticipate Mr. Brown.[50]

Moreover, Twain's reliance on Southwestern humor entails a double vision or pose. As Walter Blair and others have pointed out, many Southwestern narratives are boxlike or "framed." That is, they have an outside or "frame" narrator, usually a gentlemanly, well-educated outsider, who sets the scene and introduces the "inside" narrator, usually a colorful rustic who speaks a quaint local dialect. The inside narrator then relates a humorous anecdote. A classic example is Thorpe's "The Big Bear of Arkansas," with the anonymous outside narrator introducing us to the inside narrator, Jim Doggett. Twain's most notable use of this form is in "The Notorious Jumping Frog of Calaveras County," where the educated, somewhat pompous frame narrator introduces Simon Wheeler, who tells the story. In short, a common narrative pattern of Southwestern humor involves an outsider-insider, gentleman-rustic polarity. Moreover, as Blair notes, there is often an incongruity between the realism of the framework setting presented by the gentlemanly narrator and the tall tale related by the rustic narrator. This split between realism and fantasy might appeal to Twain, given his simultaneous realistic and romantic views. In *Mark Twain and Southwestern Humor*, Kenneth S. Lynn argues that Twain eventually fuses gentleman and rustic into one persona, a mixed self, thereby relinquishing the superiority of the gentleman to the rustic.[51] I would add that in his early writings, though, Twain tends to split these roles—for example, he assigns the role of gentleman to himself and the role of clown to Brown. Such splitting reinforces our impression that Twain is presenting highly polarized views of the world.

By sometimes limiting his role severely, Twain gains structure and stability, though at the expense of freedom and play. After all, a tightly circumscribed persona does give him an identity: in the Twain-Brown dualism of the Sandwich Islands correspondence, Twain is, quite simply, a gentleman. He typically does not let himself have any views that would be "inappropriate" for a sentimental, somewhat pretentious American bourgeois traveler. Sordid or cynical viewpoints are given to the fictitious Mr. Brown.

It is fitting that Mr. Brown comes into his own in the Sandwich Islands letters, because the Sandwich Islands pose even sharper incongruities for Twain than does the American West. As Branch notes, the islands were "a topsy-turvy, extravagant land where wonders were ready-made. Opportunities for self-display and striking contrasts were irresistible."[52] Twain finds a paradise whose beaches are littered with bones, a place of both refuge and death; the form of "self-display" he chooses is a polarization between himself and Brown. Through Brown, Twain can express many earthy and controversial views, setting up a constant conflict between gentleman Twain and barbarian Brown. Brown shows what may happen when one is stripped of romantic imagination, when realism is pushed too far and one sees with a completely unsentimental eye. When Twain offers a paean to the beauty and peace of the islands, Brown complains about the heat, cockroaches, scorpions, centipedes with "every foot hot enough to burn a hole through a raw-hide," mosquitoes so bloodthirsty that they suck him "dry as a life-preserver," and a spider so big he can "straddle over a saucer." Twain's comment? "I don't like to be interrupted when I am writing—especially by Brown, who is one of those men who always looks at the unpleasant side of everything, and I seldom do."[53] Brown undercuts every romantic view of life in the islands, while Twain struggles to maintain such views. At every turn Brown is unsentimental, uncompromising, and ungrammatical.

Twain's response to his alter ego ranges from exasperation to condescension. Twain often considers Brown young and ignorant, referring to him as "lad" or even "poor infant." At times Brown is seen as subhuman, a frontier barbarian of the lowest order. Brown is frequently presented as helpless, as when he tosses and turns with seasickness and can be cured only by exposure to Twain's poetry: "As

I finished, Brown's stomach cast up its contents, and in a minute or two he felt entirely relieved and comfortable."[54] At such times Twain seems master, Brown little better than a dog.

Yet Twain is not entirely superior to Brown. After all, Brown's vomiting in response to Twain's poetry (a rendering into rhymed quatrains of Polonius's advice to Laertes) is an appropriate answer. Twain can seem self-important and sententious when talking to Brown, like Polonius talking to Laertes. And often it is Brown, not Twain, who is unto his own self true, presenting the more discerning views of life. Brown is correct to point out that tropical islands have heat and humidity and things that crawl and bite in the night. And if Brown is ungrammatical and unsentimental, his language does at times have a fitting "poetry" of its own. His description of the coconut palm as "a feather-duster struck by lightning" is more apt than any image any writer with poetic aspirations, including Twain, is likely to present. Twain denounces Brown's cynicism, yet concedes to him many penetrating views of things. Brown's earthiness lets him see what others are blind to; he anticipates Huck Finn in his direct views. Moreover, Brown, the "poor infant," projects Twain's ambivalent feelings about childhood, with its mixture of insight and naïveté, honesty and crudity. Brown helps prepare for Mark Twain's study of another "barbarian": the boy Samuel Clemens of Hannibal.

Brown's remarks are often pointed and funny, replete with frontier vitality. Nevertheless, Twain's use of Brown leads to predictability: if Twain praises something, Brown disparages it. Such predictability prohibits inventive, versatile humor. Confined to the role of gentleman, Twain is denied the play of comic perspective he achieves in his best sketches. Twain does gain some structure through dualism, whether that dualism be expressed as between himself and another character—Brown, for example—or as entirely within a divided persona. Such dualism offers a sharp debate over the value of life, expressed as opposing (extreme) positions. But dualism, however expressed, does not do justice to Twain, for it does not permit full range to his humor and presentation of life. Life is both beautiful and ugly, and many shades in-between. To try to reduce life to labels or oppositions seems small-spirited. At his wide-ranging best, forsaking dualities, Twain indicates that life is not "positive" or "negative," not a set of charged polarities, but instead is kaleidoscopic, best imaged forth by a kaleidoscopic Twain.

Thus, Twain is usually not well served by simple dualities. In his freest, highest humor, he reveals the limitations of dualities and works to transcend them. Even in his Sandwich Islands letters, Twain sometimes blurs the line between Brown and himself, suggesting the artificiality of distinctions and trying to encompass more views. At times Twain expresses thoughts that, if he kept the duality intact, should be Brown's. For instance, Twain says, "The red sun looked across the placid ocean through the tall, clean stems of the coconut trees, like a blooming whiskey bloat through the bars of a city prison." In this case, beauty and ugliness commingle comically. Twain is as uncompromising as Brown when he gives an account of Captain Cook that undercuts the customary romantic narratives. Twain states it with all of Brown's directness but with better grace and grammar: "Plain unvarnished history takes the romance out of Captain Cook's assassination, and renders a deliberate verdict of justifiable homicide."[55] Twain incorporates Brown's straightforwardness while adding compassion for the mistreated islanders and a sense of justice; he becomes a persona who is direct without vulgarity.

We've seen that Twain usually restricts himself to the role of gentleman in the Sandwich Islands letters. In other writings, Twain experiments with defining himself by adopting various other roles, often in sharply limited ways. Branch considers that Twain frequently loses his identity "in a maze of comic poses."[56] But it might be more accurate to suggest that Twain *seeks* an identity, however mistakenly, by experimenting with different ways of restricting himself. That is, Twain seeks definition through restriction, limiting himself to a particular role in a given piece. He takes a particular aspect of his literary personality (say, the sentimental) and renders it, usually in exaggerated form, as though it were *all* that he is (in this case, a sentimentalist). John C. Gerber outlines some of the roles Twain assumes: Twain's "superior poses" (in which he presents himself as superior to the world) include gentleman, sentimentalist, instructor, and moralist; his "inferior poses" (in which he presents himself as helpless) include sufferer, simpleton, and tenderfoot. According to Gerber, each pose gives Twain "psychic support," distancing him from life's anxieties and giving him a limited point of view that "simplified life and made it more tolerable."[57] Gerber is engaging in debatable psychological analysis of Samuel Clemens, not just discussing a literary personality. If we confine ourselves to the persona and implied author, Mark Twain, we see that in adopting a specific role Twain simplifies not only how he presents life but also how he himself is presented. The problem is that such simplification does not do justice. A strategy predicated upon limitation and evasion is not likely to succeed; the sustained, conscious adoption of a set role may seem strained and artificial. Instead of being one natural attitude among many in a dynamic Mark Twain, the pose may become a fixed mask.

Moreover, the poses outlined by Gerber show a dualism between superiority and inferiority. When adopting a "superior pose," Twain suggests life is not as bad as it seems and can be mastered; when adopting an "inferior pose," Twain indicates life is much worse than it seems and overpowers one. This dualism, similar to the Twain-Brown duality, shows Twain's debate over life's value. Whenever he becomes enmeshed in this debate, Twain's views tend to polarize and rigidify; whenever he becomes too preoccupied with life's (fixed) "meaning," his humor loses its sportiveness and versatility.

Fortunately, Twain doesn't restrict himself to any given role for long; he does not harden into a permanent, narrow identity. Furthermore, by adopting diverse roles, Twain *is* exploring different ways of looking at the world and playing with possible forms of self-expression. Each role, however unsatisfactory in itself, contributes to a multifaceted and slowly evolving Twain, enabling him to play easily with many viewpoints. Each role lets him test, if in artificial and magnified form, a given perspective or mood. We witness Twain experimenting with himself as a literary personality, though he sometimes limits himself to set roles in these early writings. After all, journalism is by nature episodic and disconnected, without an overall pattern. Even in *The Innocents Abroad*, based on journalistic letters, Twain is occasionally plagued by fragmentation. Such discontinuity can easily lead to the serial adoption of certain roles, with each role controlling a given piece or episode. Only in *Roughing It*, his first book written *as* a book, does Twain become wholly versatile and fluid.

Nevertheless, Twain's experiments in these early pieces indicate well the shape of things to come. Twain suggests how intricate "identity" is and how one may experiment with it for fun or serious purposes. Life is incongruous, and often so are the roles one adopts, as Twain notes when describing a masquerade ball at New York's Academy of Music. He dresses up as a king, but feels like "a highly ornamental butcher"; he remarks on discrepancies everywhere:

> If everybody else felt as solemn and absurd as I did, they have my sympathy. . . . Dukes and princes, and queens and fairies met me at every turn, and I might have managed to imagine myself in a land of enchantment, but for remarks I was constantly overhearing. For instance, I heard Joan of Arc say she would give the world for a mess of raw oysters, and Martin Luther said he didn't feel well, because he had been playing poker for the last forty-eight hours. . . . I even heard the Queen of the Fairies say she wished she had some cheese. These little things have a tendency to destroy the pleasant illusions created by deceptive costumes.[58]

The journalist who would be king had better be careful not to become tripped up in his own play robes. Twain wrestles, albeit whimsically, with problems of roles and imaginative projections of himself. Poses may let him playfully express or exaggerate various sides of himself, but at what point do poses degenerate into nonsense or, worse yet, render him little better than a poseur? How can Twain be protean yet have integrity? If he does not fit into some conventional niche or assume some set identity, is he in danger of dissipating? Twain tells about being confronted in the Sandwich Islands by a man who is flabbergasted to find that Twain is not a whaling man, a missionary, or a government official (the three primary occupations of white men in the islands). The man asks, "Then, who the mischief are you?"[59] Whether Samuel Clemens was actually beset by such a question is debatable; but Mark Twain presents himself in many narratives as troubled by the question of identity.

A particular identity may, however, undercut itself. In a letter for the *San Francisco Daily Alta California* from New York, Twain comments on P. T. Barnum's museum and simultaneously plays the role of philosopher. Discussing the freakish sights, Twain feels sorry for a monkey whose tail has been bitten off by another monkey and who falls whenever he tries to use his nonexistent tail to grab a beam: "Why cannot he become a philosopher? Why cannot he console himself with the reflection that tails are but a delusion and a vanity at best?"[60] The irony is that the consolations of philosophy may themselves be "but a delusion and a vanity at best." Twain adopts the role of philosopher only to discover that it fails. We recall his discontent with the masquerade ball, where he laments that "Martin Luther" is under the weather after a long bout of poker. The Martin Luther role fails just as surely as the philosopher role. Twain's mood here, he confesses, is "solemn and absurd." Granted, Twain does generate some humor in these comments, but he seems to harden once more into a preoccupation with the merit of life, applying dogmatic tests for "truth" or "reality." The philosopher's position is untrue; "Martin Luther" is unreal. The implicit worry, of course, is that "Mark Twain" is also unreal. And Mark Twain is indeed unreal—there is no such human being. He is but the image that we have of Samuel Clemens. Yet as persona and implied author, Twain may be "real" within the context of his narrative worlds; he conveys the impression of vitality so long as he is dynamic and does not imprison himself within a fixed or arbitrary role. The philosopher fails because he insists upon seeing life only in stoical terms. "Martin Luther" fails because a man puts on a mask and tries to be a character that in no way expresses himself.

A role is a form of play; a pose is an attitude. Any limited form of play, any one attitude, is bound to be inadequate; reality cannot be encompassed by such narrow terms. Furthermore, any role that the player cannot *enter into* or *become* (that is, make a manifestation of himself) is bound to fail even as a partial representation of life. To succeed, Twain must metamorphose into other forms or roles; he must enter and exit each role easily, yet make each role expressive—or creative—of himself. That is, he needs to be a dynamic, highly dramatized literary personality, exhibiting a play of characteristics, each of which can naturally and readily be bodied forth as particular roles or "selves." When Twain projects this variety and does not commit himself to a fixed identity, then he presents himself—and life—richly and humorously.

The past would seem to be the greatest fixity of all: it is supposedly what is dead and done with, what has made and defined (lim-

ited) oneself. But Twain renders the past fluid. He produces a burlesque biography of Virginia City Marshal John Perry, altering Perry's
past and identity entirely. Twain transmutes Perry into a former
Commodore, Commissioner to Japan, inventor of "Perry's Pain
Killer," poet, congressman, and, significantly, actor.[61] Twain makes
Perry into a cosmos—what he himself is gradually evolving into.
Perry becomes an actor with many roles, yet Twain is the stage
manager, playing with the identities of others and himself. His cre-
ative rewriting of Perry's past anticipates what he will later do with
Samuel Clemens's past in works such as *Tom Sawyer, Life on the
Mississippi,* and *Huckleberry Finn,* as well as in an array of bur-
lesque "autobiographies" of Mark Twain.

Twain begins to play with his Hannibal past in an April 1867 letter
for the *Daily Alta California:* "Hannibal has had a hard time of it
ever since I can recollect, and I was 'raised' there. First, it had me
for a citizen, but I was too young then to really hurt the place." He
gives enlivened "reminiscences" of town drunk Jimmy Finn, a scar-
let fever epidemic, the new firehouse (which promptly burned
down), and the Cadets of Temperance. Considering a current plan
to help the town prosper by building a railroad to Moberly, Twain
doubts its success: "But won't they have to build another road to
protect the Moberly? and another and another to protect each enterprise of the kind? A railroad is like a lie—you have to keep building to it to make it stand."[62] Twain makes many of his anecdotes
stand by "building" to them. He builds upon Clemens's identity until
it can stand as that of Twain; he builds upon the identity of an entire
town until it can stand as his town. There is no preoccupation here
with facts, fixed roles, or a set identity. Ironically, the more Twain
reshapes the Hannibal past, the "truer" it becomes, the more "real"
as a town affectionately and humorously "remembered."

In addition to playing with the past, Twain considers various "transcendent figures" (to use Smith's apt term) that suggest ways for
him to grow and achieve a measure of mastery. Such figures in
Twain's early writings include Judge Shepheard and Detective Rose
in the *San Francisco Morning Call* pieces. The most notable example, however, is Captain Edgar (Ned) Wakeman, who will later
have other guises and names—Waxman, Blakely, Stormfield—in
Twain's writings.[63] Captain Wakeman, an actual person, is de-

scribed by Twain in a December 1866 letter to the *Daily Alta California:*

> I have been listening to some of Captain Waxman's [Wakeman's] stunning forecastle yarns, and I will do him the credit to say he knows how to tell them. With his strong, cheery voice, animated countenance, quaint phraseology, defiance of grammar and extraordinary vim in the matter of gesture and emphasis, he makes a most effective story out of very unpromising materials. There is a contagion about his whole-souled jollity that the chief mourner at a funeral could not resist. He is fifty years old, and as rough as a bear in voice and action, and yet as kind-hearted and tender as a woman. He is a burly, hairy, sun-burned, stormy-voiced old salt, who mixes strange oaths with incomprehensible sailor phraseology and the gentlest and most touching pathos, and is tattooed from head to foot like a Fejee Islander. His tongue is forever going when he has got no business on his hands, and though he knows nothing of policy or the ways of the world, he can cheer up any company of passengers that ever travelled in a ship, and keep them cheered up.[64]

Besides being a superb seaman, Wakeman is a marvelous story-teller whose tall tales and vigorous sea vernacular can absorb and hearten any audience—a feat immensely appealing to a writer and humorist such as Twain. Possessing the easy self-confidence of a sea god, Wakeman has many admirable qualities: he shows his good sense by marrying a runaway young couple; he displays his understanding of human nature by telling of an old woman who was disappointed to find out that a ship was not actually on fire; and, most important, he is a frontier humorist par excellence.[65] In short, Wakeman is a wonderful mixture of wisdom, lively vernacular, and humor. No doubt Twain embellishes Wakeman's character, transforming Wakeman into an Olympian figure and thereby projecting through him his own comic exaggerations, love of the vernacular, and values. Many of the Wakeman characteristics become part of the later Mark Twain. Wakeman also suggests ways Twain may transcend the Twain-Brown dualism. Wakeman is crude, ungrammatical, assertive, and strangely innocent, just like Brown; yet Wakeman is humane, imaginative, and perceptive. In some ways Wakeman is a gigantic child: like Brown and the infant terrors in "Those Blasted

Children," he represents yet another Twainian projection of "uncivilized" childhood. He is, however, a child who sees and knows much—a characteristic that will later be incorporated into Huck Finn. Perhaps most important, Wakeman seems unconcerned with set roles or with others' perceptions of him. He is free and various; one attitude melts easily into another. He may be "rough as a bear" yet "kind-hearted and tender as a woman"; he may be "stormy-voiced" yet capable of the "gentlest and most touching pathos." He is not preoccupied with adopting a fixed pose or stance toward his audience. Like life itself, he simply is. He holds forth implicit suggestions for Twain's evolution, for ways to be "whole-souled."

Despite periodic retreats into dualities and fixed roles, Twain evolves into a personality with at least some of the flexibility needed to express the range of his humor and his attitudes toward the world. In *The Innocents Abroad,* Twain confronts massive cultural conflicts in the Old World. And although occasionally he seems intimidated and defensive, Twain nevertheless develops humorous responses to the challenges of the Old World encounter, and in so doing becomes a more vigorous persona. Indeed, although some problems remain, the Mark Twain of *The Innocents Abroad* will often dominate the reader's consciousness even more than the Old World does.

3

ᴄᴏᴏ

"Gazing Out over the Ocean of Time"

The Innocents Abroad

The "pleasure trip" that Samuel Clemens took to the Old World in 1867 became the basis for Mark Twain's first major work. The sightseeing experiences of Clemens are transmuted into the comic adventures of Twain in *The Innocents Abroad,* published in 1869.[1] In his narrative, Twain presents lands filled with monuments, revered artworks, and tombs—a combination of museum and graveyard. In these old lands, laid out by guidebooks and presided over by guides, Twain faces an accomplished fact: an oceanic past, deep as the centuries, wherein lies much of the notable art, religion, suffering, and thought of the human race. According to custom, he is to look upon the monuments, humble himself, extract the meaning that the guidebooks tell him is there, and thereby fix his relationship to the Old World and understand its values.

But he cannot do so, for he finds the Old World a jumble. In the murk of Europe and the Near East, as in the clear but deceptive air of the American West, Twain is bedeviled by discrepancies, hoaxes, and illusions. He faces difficulty in interpreting the incongruous Old World past, reconciling this past with the present, and presenting a coherent image of himself, the relatively "uncultured" westerner, in the face of this alien, disappointing, and threatening world. As he did with the West, Twain strives to mold the material of the Old World into manageable form. By humorously critiquing the Old World, Twain denies its power over him and creates alternative meanings to those prescribed by guides and customs. The flexibility of humor offers him the freedom to see new meanings in the Old World. In *The Innocents Abroad,* Twain presents himself and his adventures through the power of imaginative humor; though Twain's imagination occasionally fails before the ponderous force of the Old World, he nonetheless offers comic transformations of life that are a significant advance over his earlier narratives. Indeed, Twain successfully takes many Old World contradictions and turns them into his own brand of humorous disruption, his own play of perspective. He challenges the Old World's standards, traditions, and beliefs; he uses the power of humor to substitute his own elastic models of reality.

In its genesis and revisions *The Innocents Abroad* demonstrates the imaginative power of Twain, for it is considerably different from his newspaper correspondence. As Leon T. Dickinson, Dewey Ganzel, Daniel Morley McKeithan, Franklin Walker, and others have shown, Twain has extensively revised his newspaper letters for the book, deleting some passages, altering others, and writing new sections to provide continuity or to replace letters that had miscarried. In particular, Twain removes or tones down much of the newspaper irreverence and vulgarity. He eliminates his Mr. Hyde alter ego—the fictional character Brown. Most of Brown's remarks are deleted, though some are "given" to other passengers, real or imaginary, or voiced directly by Twain himself as he evolves into a more complex persona. Twain also eliminates much of the western dialect and many specific western references. He spruces up his grammar and vocabulary, striving to appear more "refined," reasonable, and tolerant—although he also increases his criticism of the "pilgrims," the pious, older passengers of the *Quaker City*. Finally, he makes some notable creative insertions or revisions, including the famous Adam's tomb passage, the taunting of the Italian guides, and the hymn to the Sphinx.[2] The general impression given as one turns from reading the newspaper letters to reading the book is that of moving from a brash, fragmented, fiercely irreverent western view to a more controlled narrative designed for an eastern, predominantly female audience who wanted to be entertained but not offended—who wanted illusions cracked, perhaps, but not shattered. In making these changes for his projected reading public and for his image as an urbane, cosmopolitan writer, Twain loses more than some scholars have been willing to concede. There is a primal vigor in some of the *Daily Alta California* letters unmatched in the book. But Twain also gains a more reflective, mature presentation—one that lets him raise questions about the certainty of knowledge, the past, and personal identity. The book is often less exuberant and freewheeling than the newspaper letters, but it is more balanced, expressing more sophisticated viewpoints. By asserting such viewpoints, Twain confronts with considerable success the incongruities and illusions of the Old World.

In his preface Twain confronts the experience of his "pleasure trip" and the reader himself. As in his western newspaper writing, Twain fights illusion with illusion. He suggests throughout his narrative that the "great pleasure excursion" so heralded in the newspapers and ship's prospectus was often anything but pleasurable; but here he pretends it was a "pic-nic." In addition to recording his trip, he indicates a simple, refreshing purpose: "to suggest to the reader how *he* would be likely to see Europe and the East if he looked at them with his own eyes instead of the eyes of those who travelled in those countries before him." Twain sets illusions against one another, triggering dissonance that might encourage the reader to question the narrative's purpose. If the reader accepts the notion that the trip was a picnic, he is left to wonder what to make of the assertion that he should see (through Twain's eyes) the Old World for himself, not as it has been described, usually glowingly, by previous travelers. Twain intimates that Europe and the East are not what they are cracked up to be, that he who sees with his own eyes will be disillusioned—and surely disillusionment is no picnic. Caught in this contradiction, the reader becomes entangled: how can *he* see the Old World for himself through Twain's eyes? Twain certainly knows about this problem, for in Venice he remarks, apropos of how his evaluation of famous paintings differs from that of other tourists, "can I see them through others' eyes?" (23). In *The Innocents Abroad* the reader sees Twain's image of pictures and places—an image that may be more entertaining, instructive, and complex than that presented by the guidebooks, but Twain's image nonetheless. Many a reader (especially eastern readers trained to admire European culture) might not entirely share Twain's brash and unorthodox perspective, even while finding that perspective enjoyable. Moreover, even if the reader is unacquainted with Twain's western reputation as the "Moralist of the Main" and his tendency to convert personal views into ethical imperatives, the reader may wonder how description can avoid becoming prescription. Twain may pretend to have "seen with impartial eyes," but the reader may be pardoned for wondering how anyone, least of all Twain, can be so impartial since the self is subjective by nature.[3] And Twain's humor revels in the subjective. In short, the preface reminds the reader that the narrative is Mark Twain's: the narrative presents Twain, in his array of stances and attitudes as a multiform persona, far more than it presents any "objective" view of the Old World.

Through this playful preface, Twain encourages the reader to confront some of the same epistemological issues the narrative itself confronts: to what extent can one *know* something? What is one to do in a world of illusions where no one is a truly objective, independent observer? Twain's dynamic narrative is replete with conflict: change versus stability, multiplicity versus unity, sordid realism versus romantic dream, the objective versus the subjective. Twain brilliantly exposes layer upon layer of incongruity and irony, suggesting how little "solid reality" there is for him (or the reader) to latch onto. From the Azores to Palestine, Twain suggests that the Old World—and life in general—is founded upon increasingly elaborate illusions and deceptions.

As in his western pieces, Twain presents himself as bewildered by a disorienting world. His narrative suggests that he sets out innocently on the excursion. Enticed by newspaper publicity about the *Quaker City* cruise, the first American pleasure voyage of its kind, he understands neither the nature of the trip nor his fellow passengers; only the trip itself can teach him. One irony is the attempt to find pleasure in the monuments of the past—a past filled with squalor and suffering incomprehensible to the prosperous passengers of the *Quaker City,* a past still haunting many of the places Twain visits. One wonders how anyone can approach that history in the mood of a "pleasure excursion." Moreover, any bucket lowered into the past is likely to bring up tears. When Twain later examines an ancient Etruscan tear jug near Pisa, he notes:

> It spoke to us in a language of its own; and with a pathos more tender than any words might bring, its mute eloquence swept down

the long roll of the centuries with its tale of a vacant chair, a familiar footstep missed from the threshold, a pleasant voice gone
from the chorus, a vanished form!—a tale which is always so new
to us, so startling, so terrible, so benumbing to the senses, and behold how threadbare and old it is! (24)

It is the tale of the past, preserved in the museum of the Old World,
speaking of death and of the frustration of human hopes. Similar
to the West's "tragical strain," the Old World's pathos challenges
Twain's capacity for response and representation.

From this central irony spring others. Sailing aboard a ship named
for the city of brotherly love, Twain seeks joy and camaraderie but
instead finds discord. "Pilgrims" are pitted against "sinners" (Twain
and some of the younger, more fun-loving passengers); throughout
his narrative Twain complains about the boring devotions that pre-
vail aboard the ship. The setting forth of the *Quaker City* is beset
by ill omens: a storm rages outside the harbor; the ship's "gallant
flag" hangs "limp and disheartened by the spectacle"; and the shore
battery that is supposed to boom out a farewell is silent because
"the ammunition was out." The whole bedraggled scene leads Twain
to remark drily, "This was pleasuring with a vengeance" (2). *The Innocents Abroad* cleverly indicates not only the confusion that the
Americans encounter abroad but also the discords they carry within
themselves. Indeed, Twain and his fellow passengers are sometimes
the most outlandish spectacle to be seen abroad. Twain suggests
that outer incongruities echo inner ones; *The Innocents Abroad* is
not only about foreign lands seen but also about seers seen, including, most of all, Twain himself. As Ganzel points out, the focus is on
the literary consciousness we call Mark Twain.[4] And this focus increasingly discovers Twain's complexities as he develops responses
to the Old World.

Crossing the Atlantic, the *Quaker City* reveals its discords and
disorientations. Seasickness reigns; the ship seems ruled by five
"captains," each of whom takes Twain to task for the slightest in-
fraction; an attempt to play "horse billiards" results only in helpless
reeling; passengers begin journals, only to leave them incomplete;
pilgrims square off against sinners; an effort at music and dancing
ends in discordant noise with the dancers thrown from one side of

the ship to the other; a mock trial produces witnesses who are "stupid, and unreliable and contradictory, as witnesses always are," not to mention lawyers who are "vindictively abusive of each other" and a judge who issues "an absurd decision and a ridiculous sentence." Finally, there is the subtle suggestion that discord prevails not just in human nature or in stormy weather, but in the very scheme of things. What is a "fair wind" for one ship (the pilgrims pray for a favorable wind for the *Quaker City*) is a foul wind for all ships headed in the opposite direction (3, 4). Twain suggests that disharmony is the condition of existence and that such dysfunction can be tolerated only by a humorous observer.

Thus far, Twain seems to preserve his equilibrium as tourist and narrator. He does not suffer from seasickness and works regularly at his journal and letters, as he is paid to do. When "Blucher," one of Twain's comic creations based on an actual passenger, complains that his watch no longer keeps "good time" no matter how much he pushes up the "regulator," Twain sends him to the captain for an explanation of "ship time" (5).[5] Twain's easy answer to Blucher's problem might suggest that Twain's own "regulator" is working well. But the discords that begin confronting him quickly show his own disorders, his own maladjusted regulator. Just as Blucher can't match his idea of time as something fixed and universal with actual ship time, so Twain finds that he sometimes can't match his idea of the Old World with what he experiences.

Time begins to afflict Twain, too. Throughout the trip he will be awakened at odd hours for odd reasons. At the Azores he is rousted out at 5:30 A.M. to go onto a cold, windy deck to stare at an island in the fog. Periodically during the excursion Twain suggests he is in a fog, the victim of constant traveling, disruption of sleep, and a demanding writing schedule. *The Innocents Abroad* presents a consciousness sometimes off balance, confused, and tired, especially toward the end.

At the Azores, Twain joins Blucher in disorientation. His first problem is the difference between American and Portuguese currency; Twain himself believes that a dinner party bill of 21,700 reis represents a fortune (it represents $21.70). Twain is caught out because he puts the same faith in the supposed absolute value of money that Blucher puts in the supposed absolute value of time. As his narrative suggests, the Old World demands new perspectives, a new relativism, if Twain is to maintain his equilibrium.

His disorientation worsens once Twain and his fellow passengers reach Europe and begin the expedition in earnest. For Twain, the incongruities are of three kinds: the difficulty of reconciling American values with those abroad; the discrepancies between images proffered by guidebooks (or by one's own romantic imagination) and sordid reality; and the longing for the eternal constantly scraping up against the horrors of mutability. Moreover, there is the unnerving sense that what is found on this excursion exemplifies the jumble of experience. As in his western journalism, Twain details the many puzzles he faces, thereby emphasizing—and dramatizing—the ordeal he must undergo. Indeed, Twain sets up this excursion as a testing ground, an arduous challenge he must master through humor and reason. It is an excursion not just into the Old World but also into Twain. On one level, Twain, still evolving as a persona, suggests the need to test and exert his comic powers; on another level, his narrative suggests the efforts of every mind to transform a recalcitrant and problematic reality into some order.

The Innocents Abroad is often read as a confrontation between the New World and the Old World, a humorous and uncouth man's version of a Henry James narrative. Twain does partly shape his narrative from this perspective: an innocent, an American Adam, goes up against the sophistication and shams of the Old World. Although there is much to quarrel with in this picture (the passengers, including Twain, are not exactly simple, harmonious Adams but are divided among and within themselves), such an approach does let Twain reemphasize the incongruities and challenges he faces. As John C. McCloskey notes, Twain often "gawks like any other tourist."[6] By presenting himself this way, Twain suggests how easily the Old World may sometimes awe and even overwhelm him.

Twain is careful, however, not to enact another characteristic generally associated with the American Adam: boorishness. Twain presents an ugly American who reveals his ignorance at every turn, orders about a French waiter, and loudly proclaims, "I am a free-born sovereign, sir, an American, sir, and I want everybody to know it!" Twain wryly remarks, "He did not mention that he was a lineal descendant of Balaam's ass; but everybody knew that without his telling" (11). This unexpected and devastating association, characteristic of his humor, lets Twain take the moral high road. *His* American Adam is usually innocent without being boorish. Though often caught in discords and mistakes, Twain seems superior to the typical American tourist, if only because of his amused acknowledgment of his own naïveté.

Mark Twain follows this passage by describing a visit to the Marseilles zoo—a visit that, as Robert Regan notes, probably never actually occurred since Samuel Clemens and his companions were pressed for time and not near the zoo.[7] If so, the reader is not "seeing" anything for himself but rather is presented with fabrication, a visit to a scene that may bear little or no resemblance to reality, a visit paid by Twain's imagination. Among the creatures at the zoo, Twain describes "a sort of tall, long-legged bird with a beak like a powder-horn and close-fitting wings like the tails of a dress coat" (11). This bird, with his "tranquil stupidity," "supernatural gravity," "self-righteousness," and "ineffable self-complacency," symbolizes one type of American: the "pilgrim." This pious, hypocritical, hymn-singing species, native to Henry Ward Beecher's Plymouth Congregational Church and other such places, Twain finds in abundance aboard the *Quaker City.* Twain satirizes this ungainly creature for his arrogance, gullibility, and thoughtless cruelty. Throughout his narrative Twain chides the pilgrims for their conceit that American English should be spoken everywhere, that American Protestantism is the one true faith, and that America is the standard by which all other countries are to be measured. He lampoons them for their desecration of monuments and inveterate relic-hunting (one chips away at the face of the Sphinx). "Vandals," Twain calls the proud and plundering Americans. He carefully distinguishes his reflections from the unreflecting barbarisms of most American tourists. Also, by hitting at the pilgrims' "supernatural gravity" and "ineffable self-complacency," Twain indicates their most important failing: lack of humor. Taking themselves too seriously, they lack the flexibility to face an alien world. In contrast, Twain's humor is often self-disparaging, which means he is willing to adjust himself as circumstances warrant. Twain may at times make as big a fool out of himself as the pilgrims do, but he does it with better grace and humor; unlike the pilgrims, he sees neither world nor self as a sacred fixity. The typical pilgrim, resembling the bird at the Marseilles zoo, is fixed in place; Twain is a bird in flight.

Whether tossed about by their donkeys in the Azores, straggling like an American Indian tribe through Gibraltar, or riding horses in Palestine, the Americans are often the silliest spectacle in the land. As Twain comments in his final chapter, "The people stared at us everywhere." He adds, "If ever those children of Israel in Palestine forget when Gideon's Band went through there from America, they ought to be cursed once more and finished. It was the rarest spectacle that ever astounded mortal eyes, perhaps" (61). Ironically compounding this absurdity is the fact that the Americans, voyaging to stare upon the wonders of a dead past, are sometimes seen by the Old World as bringing death themselves. At times they are quarantined because it is feared that they bring cholera, that they are a ship not only of fools but also of death.

But if Twain presents Americans as walking absurdities, he presents Europeans and Middle Easterners in an equally ludicrous light. Everywhere the Americans are beset by grubby, ignorant, self-satisfied guides eager to part the American fool from his money. In Paris they are led by a guide into every possible shop so that they might spend their money, when what they want is to go to the Louvre. At the Great Pyramid they are importuned by Arabs who want to haul them up and down the pyramid, wrenching their bones out of place. At every turn Twain is shown artworks and relics that he either cannot appreciate or suspects are shams. He is surrounded by beggars and cripples, particularly in Constantinople, where the human exhibits present a P. T. Barnum show of human deformity and misery (33). The beggars, especially the Arab beggars, appall him; Ganzel notes that to Twain they seem subhuman, beggars by choice, and so he has little sympathy for them.[8] No doubt Twain applies the American Protestant work ethic and thinks the beggars are impoverished by sloth; he compares them to American Indians, whom he also routinely brands as lazy and shiftless. If America for Twain is the land of ignorance, gullibility, and nervous bustling, Europe and the Middle East are pigsties.

When worlds collide, both are shattered. In *The Innocents Abroad,* Twain's overall attitude toward the New World and the Old World is "a plague on both your houses." Thus, he notes that riches in America serve the same purpose as noble birth in Europe—to exalt the stupid and contemptible (26). By taunting a Genovese guide, Twain and his friends ridicule the excessive European admiration for "relics"—in this case, anything associated with Columbus, including one of his letters. But they do so by humorously exaggerating the Franklinian principle that in America it is not who you are but what you can do that matters. "The doctor," an occasional spokesman for Twain's skepticism and in some respects a Brown stand-in, decries the poor penmanship of the letter: "We are not fools by a good deal. If you have got any specimens of penmanship of real merit, trot them out! And if you haven't, drive on!" (27). The consequence is that both European and American attitudes appear ridiculous. Twain seems satisfied neither with the fixity and reverence of the Old World nor with the fluidity and irreverence of the New World.

Because of this alienation from both worlds, Twain cannot be rooted in either context, as Whitman is in the New World or James is in the Old World. By contrasting and lampooning the two worlds in detail, Twain cuts himself adrift. He has to evolve from his own humor, not from any given cultural context. This prompts Twain to experiment with self-development and expression so that, even while he pokes fun at himself, he rises above both Old World and New World. At his best, Twain becomes his own world. But Twain's remoteness from Europe and America, his wandering in a void, also increases his risk of instability. Moreover, he cannot just contrast the Old World with the New World, scoff at both, and be done. His narrative suggests conflicts that represent not simply a matter of opposing cultures but basic epistemological and psychological problems he needs to accommodate.

Such problems are implied in his anecdote about a tree in a Parisian park:

> It was in this park that that fellow with an unpronounceable name made the attempt upon the Russian Czar's life last spring with a pistol. The bullet struck a tree. Ferguson showed us the place. Now in America that interesting tree would be chopped down or forgotten within the next five years, but it will be treasured here. The guides will point it out to visitors for the next eight hundred years, and when it decays and falls down they will put up another there and go on with the same old story just the same. (14)

Twain lampoons the European compulsion to preserve the past, but he also implies a touch of contempt for America because of its short memory and ruthless drive toward the future. Samuel Clemens was an avid student of the past; his personal library at the time of his death numbered many volumes of history and biography, from Plutarch to Parkman.[9] As Mark Twain, he may decry the mustiness and trickery of the Old World, but he cannot deny the need for a sense of historical continuity. Twain suggests an incongruity that goes much deeper than the confrontation of the Old World with the New World. *The Innocents Abroad* suggests that one must obliterate much of the past, historical and personal, in order to change and move toward the future; yet one must also preserve some awareness of the past, somehow keep it "real," if one is to have a sense of continuity and identity. In short, one needs both change and stasis—a problem that must be solved if experience is to be ordered. Twain is careful to present himself as free and innovative yet aware of the vast force of history. Even a volatile Twain needs to be related to the past in some way. Twain cannot present himself as completely cut off from the history of art, aspiration, and suffering. Yet he also needs the fluidity not to be fixed by that past. He must not let past conceptions of life become unduly restrictive, or his humor—and his narrative—will falter. It is by incorporating both past and present, tradition and innovation, that Twain becomes a richer, more sophisticated literary personality.

Twain also strives to reconcile some other polarities, including order versus chaos, unity versus multiplicity, and especially romance versus reality. Such problems likewise transcend the motif of Old World versus New World and point to fundamental difficulties in experience, for they question how one is to fit ideals to experience. In *The Innocents Abroad* these problems commonly take the form of a discrepancy between what Twain expects to see and what he does see.

Indeed, Twain expects to see a great deal. Despite his cynicism, Twain displays an earnest search for spectacle and significance. He is always eager to set off on more side trips, more midnight excursions, as though seeking some order that will give meaning to what he sees and set the world right. Granted, his book's subtitle, *The New Pilgrims' Progress,* is ironic, and various expressions (such as "this European exodus," chapter 2) play satirically off biblical notions of a journey to a promised land. Twain indicates as well that this voyage will not lead to any promised land: a magic-lantern show is prefaced by the exhibitor's remark that he wants to "show the passengers where they shall eventually arrive" and then he mistakenly shows them a cemetery (4). Nevertheless, Twain has great expectations. When disappointed by the shams and confusions of the Old World, he reacts strongly, questioning the value of experience. Such disappointments test his capacity for flexible, humorous response.

As many readers have noted, *The Innocents Abroad* frequently demonstrates romantic illusions, fostered by innocence or distance, yielding to disappointment as Twain gains experience or a closer look. Forrest G. Robinson points out that Twain describes places such as Venice as beautiful at a distance but as ugly close-up.[10] The effect reminds us of how Twain praises the Sandwich Islands and Brown disparages them—a simplistic pattern of dream and disillusionment. For Montaigne, "to know all is to forgive all"; but often for Twain, the more he knows about places and people, the more disappointed he becomes. Like Gulliver among the Brobdingnagians, he finds that close inspection reveals warts, pores, and blemishes.[11] Dreams and pictures promote only illusions, as he notes in his description of Constantinople:

> Seen from the anchorage or from a mile or so up the Bosporus, it is by far the handsomest city we have seen. Its dense array of houses swell upward from the water's edge, and spreads over the domes of many hills; and the gardens that peep out here and there, the great globes of the mosques, and the countless minarets that meet the eye every where, invest the metropolis with the quaint Oriental aspect one dreams of when he reads books of eastern travel. Constantinople makes a noble picture.
> But its attractiveness begins and ends with its picturesqueness. From the time one starts ashore till he gets back again, he execrates it. The boat he goes in is admirably miscalculated for the service it is built for. . . . You start to go to a given point and you run in fifty different directions before you get there. (33)

Ashore, Twain finds beggars, cripples, dogs, and filth. He does generate some humor amid this misery and absurdity: "Ashore it was—well, it was an eternal circus. People were thicker than bees in those narrow streets, and the men were dressed in all the outrageous, outlandish, idolatrous, extravagant, thunder-and-lightning costumes that ever a tailor with the delirium tremens and seven devils could conceive of." And he has funny and bright remarks on the slave-girl markets, Turkish baths, ubiquitous dogs, and scarcity of morals and whiskey. But at times he sounds disillusioned, his humor forced—especially when he is reduced to making jokes about human deformities and the dirt in the mosque of St. Sophia. Like the Turkish boat, his humor here is "admirably miscalculated" to take him anywhere, and he is left rudderless and adrift. Play has degenerated into confusion; nothing seems true to him. The guidebooks lie; dreams lie; pictures lie. Dreams and pictures project human wishes, not reality. In Egypt, Twain finds that even the Great Pyramid, the only surviving "wonder" of the ancient world, is beautiful only at a hazy distance. Up close "it was a fairy vision no longer. It was a corrugated, unsightly mountain of stone" (58).

For Twain, such disillusionment challenges tradition, authority, and belief. Like Melville's Redburn, who has his father's old guidebook to Liverpool but finds that it doesn't match the city, Twain doesn't lack for guidebooks but finds that most have only a passing acquaintance with reality. He is left questioning and frustrated. Early in the narrative Twain introduces a passenger, "young and green, and not bright, not learned and not wise," whom Twain nicknames the "Interrogation Point" because he is always asking naïve questions (7). The questions Twain raises are usually more thoughtful, but, like the "Interrogation Point," he is generally eager and curious. And like the Interrogation Point, Twain rarely seems to get satisfactory answers to his questions. He presents himself as often unable to make sense of things; though Twain celebrates a play of perspective in his narrative, he also suggests through repeated exasperation just how unsettling the lack of any answer, any "truth," may be. Indeed, his response sometimes is a Brown-like lapse into narrow cynicism, reinforcing a rigid romanticism-realism dichotomy (romantic Twain versus disillusioned Twain).

He is clearly dissatisfied with Leonardo da Vinci's *The Last Supper,* which he sees as a faded old humbug, sadly the worse for wear thanks to time and the kicks of Napoleon's Philistine horses. Surveying the openmouthed adulation of onlookers, Twain wonders,

"How can they see what is not visible?" (19). He later characterizes this phenomenon as guidebook mentality: one sees what one expects to see or has been told to see. Twain implicitly raises the question of how any truth can be attained when such misperceptions occur. He discusses the inability of people to "read" accurately the facial expressions of even the most talented actor, suggesting the innate subjectivity and deceitfulness of perception and experience (19). Soon afterward Twain is so frustrated by the whole business of trying to judge the aesthetic quality of celebrated paintings that he mockingly sorts paintings by subject matter, thereby implying that he is making the only "judgment" possible (23).

He is even more cynical (again, à la Brown) when facing issues involving not only aesthetics but also ethics and religious beliefs. Although his criticism of Palestine is milder here than in his letters, Twain's mockery nonetheless emerges. Allison Ensor may be right that, during his trip to Palestine, Samuel Clemens "never openly challenged the authority of the Bible on an important matter"[12]— but Mark Twain is dissatisfied with the land, its peoples, and various Christian traditions and legends. Some disappointments may seem minor (and intentionally comic), as when he laments that Palestinian grapes are not nearly as large as in Sunday school pictures or when he grouses that the Jordan is a rather small river (42, 55). But for Twain, almost *everything* in Palestine is smaller, less significant, and more sordid than he had anticipated. "I must begin a system of reduction," he declares; Palestine cramps him (46). The mean huts frescoed with camel dung, the gray, monotonous desolation, the fly-infested beggars crying for "baksheesh," the quarreling of religious sects at the Church of the Holy Sepulchre, and the outlandish legends that insult one's intelligence all leave Twain disillusioned. He exposes human gullibility, but some of his humor seems predictable, not protean: he sets up cherished conceptions, only to knock them down. That is, at times Twain oscillates routinely between the poles of romantic illusion and cynical realism. Indeed, the reader sometimes anticipates what Twain's attitude toward a given subject will be, so predictable do Twain's responses become at times. On such occasions Twain does not do justice to the variety and wonder of life; toward the end of his trip he sounds increasingly tired and disappointed with what he sees.

Twain retreats into this pattern because quite a bit of Palestine, and the Old World generally, is incomprehensible to him—and perhaps rightly so, in the judgment of numerous perceptive readers who likewise find much of the Old World a baffling amalgam of tradition, fraud, and illusion. In any event, Twain presents himself as someone who can no more understand what he sees—or other tourists' reaction to it—than he can understand the foreign languages. His anecdote about how he cannot explain one of his jokes to customs officials at Rome, with the result that they "confiscate" it as being possibly dangerous (25), is a paradigm for what befalls him throughout the trip. By using a pattern of predictable responses on occasion, Twain provides himself with stability and structure amid the Old World's confusions, but at the expense of creativity, fluidity, and a humor that might transcend (or at least play with) absurd or ironic situations.

Like his western articles, *The Innocents Abroad* thus lapses sometimes into polarities and fixed responses. But at his best—and that includes much of his narrative—Twain experiments with many perspectives; the disappointments and frustrations of the Old World prompt him not to retreat but to develop a new flexibility and inclusiveness. For instance, he satirizes a minister for believing that "the heart of St. Philip Neri was so inflamed with divine love as to burst his ribs." Twain notes, "I find that grave statement in a book published in New York in 1858 and written by 'Rev. William H. Neligan, LL.D., M.A., Trinity College, Dublin; Member of the Archaeological Society of Great Britain.' Therefore I believe it. Otherwise I could not. Under other circumstances I should have felt a curiosity to know what Philip had for dinner" (27). But after dripping humorous sarcasm and hard logic, Twain adds, "I would gladly change my unbelief for Neligan's faith, and let him make the conditions as hard as he pleased. The old gentleman's undoubting, unquestioning simplicity has a rare freshness about it in these matter-of-fact railroading and telegraphing days." That is, Twain suggests a need for both reason and faith; though he disbelieves the legend about St. Philip, he suggests that human emotions cannot be reduced to simple logic.

Similarly, Twain questions his own tendency to reduce things sometimes to their bare essentials. In the bone-bedecked catacombs of the Capuchin Convent he meets a genial old friar who tells about a young monk who died long ago because of a tragic love affair. The friar illustrates the tale by nonchalantly pointing to various bones of the dead man. Twain notes, "This business-like way of illustrating a touching story of the heart by laying the several fragments of the lover before us and naming them, was as grotesque a performance, and as ghastly, as any I ever witnessed. I hardly knew whether to smile or shudder" (28). Yet, immediately afterward, Twain reduces Raphael's *The Transfiguration* to its physical dimensions, and aesthetic judgments to nonsense: "The colors are fresh and rich, the 'expression,' I am told, is fine, the 'feeling' is lively, the 'tone' is good, the 'depth' is profound, and the width is about four and a half feet, I should judge." The old friar could not have done it better. We do not know "whether to smile or shudder."

By placing this passage after the tale told by the Capuchin friar, Twain displays his ambivalence about how to "judge" life and art. He pokes fun at those tourists who respond to "great art" only in the prescribed terms; he may even be poking fun at Raphael, insinuating that *The Transfiguration* is not so wonderful as reputed. But Twain also engages in humorous self-depreciation by suggesting that he is sometimes as mechanical, as literal, as the old friar. In short, Twain indicates he does not know just how to consider either the friar's tale or Raphael's painting. Once again, the demands of reason and emotion are commingled, and because of this ambiguity Twain becomes more complex and varied. Modern readers are sensitive to Twain's ambivalence, themselves caught in an age that demands dry technological precision but still desiring love, art, faith. Scientific-minded but unpredictably emotional, Twain displays an array of responses to the Old World that transcends the dichotomy of romanticism and realism. Furthermore, by lampooning his own occasional tendency toward the mechanical or simplistic (a rather widespread human failing, after all), Twain suggests a degree of sophistication and self-reflection not found in most tourists.

Such successful passages help us understand another reason Twain is not well served in those instances when he relies upon set responses. There is rampant reductionism in his treatment of *The Last Supper* and Palestine; even if the painting and the land aren't as wonderful as reputed, Twain unwarrantably strips both subjects of connotations and implicit associations. That is, for many people, both subjects subtly inspire a long, intricate train of ideas and images. But Twain treats *The Last Supper* as though it were nothing more than paint upon a wall, disregarding its past, its meaning for many viewers, and its subject matter. He draws a circle around it, isolating it as would a chemist studying a new compound; his treatment of Palestine is much the same. Yet Twain knows the value of association; after all, his best humor often depends upon his conjoining one thing with another, as when he links the ugly American with Balaam's ass. Regarding the Sea of Galilee, Twain notes that its history and connotations are what matter (48). In *Roughing It* he refines his use of association in such anecdotes as "Jim Blaine and His Grandfather's Ram."[13] Versatile humor needs flexible and even free association, not limitation and fixity.

On those occasions when Twain narrows his view arbitrarily and ignores such associations, he does an injustice to his subject, his humor, and himself. Only by considering a plethora of associations (both historical and personal, given and created) for a particular subject, only by giving free play to his emotions, can Twain remedy this injustice. These associations may be ambiguous, if not incongruous; Twain's variable reactions may present him as unsettled. Nevertheless, only by being thus faithful to the puzzling variety in life is Mark Twain able to offer mature responses to the experiences of Samuel Clemens.

By exhibiting an array of attitudes, Twain transcends the role of typical tourist. Most "pilgrims" have set reactions to the Old World, based on their guidebooks, religious beliefs, and American arrogance. Their relationship to the Old World is determined, whereas Twain's is more free. But the pilgrims have the advantage of knowing who they are and what they "see," albeit in a narrow way. They are the true believers for whom all is prescribed. Conversely, Twain often has only himself to fall back upon; not surprisingly, at times he seems overwhelmed by the intricate incongruities of both the Old World and himself. He seems unsettled, vulnerable.

Sometimes Twain seems as flayed and tormented as the Phidian statue that darkly fascinates him:

> The figure was that of a man without a skin; with every vein, artery, muscle, every fibre and tendon and tissue of the human

frame, represented in minute detail. It looked natural, because somehow it looked as if it were in pain. A skinned man would be likely to look that way unless his attention were occupied with some other matter. It was a hideous thing, and yet there was a fascination about it some where. I am very sorry I saw it, because I shall always see it, now. I shall dream of it sometimes. I shall dream that it is resting its corded arms on the bed's head and looking down on me with its dead eyes; I shall dream that it is stretched between the sheets with me and touching me with its exposed muscles and its stringy cold legs. (18)

This nightmare figure staring back at him suggests Twain's fear of what may figuratively befall him. The Old World may lay him as bare as the Phidian statue. In another image of flaying, though humorously presented, Twain claims to have been skinned alive by a masseur after an unpleasant Turkish bath. "It is a tedious process," he tells the masseur. "It will take hours to trim me to the size you want me; I will wait; go and borrow a jack-plane" (34).

Through such images Twain implies a fear of being whittled down to insignificance, even nothingness, by the incongruities, quandaries, and problems of experience that the Old World presents. And herein lies one explanation for what some readers may see as a puzzling incongruity in *The Innocents Abroad:* this humorous travel narrative is replete with images of suffering, entrapment, and death. Although Twain's reliance on a violent Southwestern brand of humor and the Old World's bloody past are possible causes, a more likely cause is that such images let Twain suggest a periodic feeling of helplessness before the confusions of an alien world. For instance, the motif of imprisonment runs throughout his narrative.[14] He visits the prison at Marseilles, describing its dungeons in ways that anticipate his description of Morgan le Fay's dungeons in *A Connecticut Yankee;* he crosses the Bridge of Sighs and visits the prison at Venice, meditating on how solitary imprisonment would lead to a loss of identity; and he often presents himself as a prisoner, confined by guides, guidebooks, beggars, and the monotonous round of sightseeing (11, 12, 22).[15] Like the solitary prisoner, Twain questions who he is.

Images of death reflect even more clearly his anxieties about himself and the world he confronts, for death is the ultimate helplessness. In moments of futility, Twain doesn't hesitate to apply to himself the Ecclesiastes theme that "all is vanity." He observes a desert lizard: "If he could speak, he would say, Build temples: I will lord it in their ruins; build palaces: I will inhabit them; erect empires: I will inherit them; bury your beautiful: I will watch the worms at their work: and you, who stand here and moralize over me: I will crawl over *your* corpse at the last" (47). He confronts the dead past when the broken statues lying around the Parthenon stare at him in the Athenian moonlight (32). He notes of "the tomb-like, stone-paved parlors and bed-rooms of Europe and Asia" that they "make one think of the grave all the time" (44).

Similarly, Twain's disgust with various famous paintings, statues, and monuments arises in part because they suggest the horrors and humiliations of mutability. Thus, Twain complains that some statues of apostles are "a swarm of rusty, dusty, battered apostles standing around the filigree work, some on one leg and some with two or three fingers gone, and some with not enough nose left to blow—all of them crippled and discouraged, and fitter subjects for the hospital than the cathedral" (6). We've seen his response to what the ravages of time and Napoleon's horses have done to *The Last Supper*. Granted, in such examples Twain manufactures humor from the way he describes the shabby old relics; but he seems troubled nonetheless, and a pattern is set for his later narratives. For Twain, mutability is mutilation.

Through his presentation of such issues, Twain suggests the difficulties posed by the Old World—and by life generally—and just what the demands on his humor are. Through comic narrative Twain must become more dominant than the challenges he details. Moreover, these problems bear on his presentation of the past and his difficulty in reconciling the eternal with the mutable. In *Twain and the Image of History,* Roger Salomon suggests, citing Terence Martin, that the most crucial conflict in *The Innocents Abroad* is between stasis and change.[16] As we'll see, Twain is unhappy with both timelessness and change, analogous to his dissatisfaction with both the Old World and the New World. For Twain, the conflict between stasis and change strikes deep because it concerns his development as persona. Though he fears the Old World's past as a heavy burden that might limit how he thinks and perceives, Twain also is attracted to that past as an image of stability and eternity—a reassurance amid the sometimes chaotic volatility engendered by his humor. Caught between desires for both stability and fluidity, Twain at times becomes trapped in a dichotomy of eternity and mutability, similar to the dichotomy of romanticism and realism.

Fearing transience, Twain sometimes seeks consolation in the eternal. He extols Père la Chaise, the French national cemetery, as "a solemn city [with its] mansions of the dead [that are] so exquisite in design, so rich in art, so costly in material, so graceful, so beautiful" (15). He repeats this "city of the dead" motif—a stock Victorian morbidity—in his description of the cemetery at Genoa: "On either side . . . are monuments, tombs, and sculptured figures that are exquisitely wrought and are full of grace and beauty. They are new, and snowy; every outline is perfect, every feature guiltless of mutilation, flaw or blemish" (17). Leslie Fiedler complains that Twain is pandering to the poor taste of his readers by providing them with guidebook fare: the Genoan cemetery was renowned (falsely) for its beauty and Twain capitalizes on that renown.[17] Fiedler's criticism has merit; but whatever one may think of the above quotation, Twain grapples with a basic problem here. Like Poe, he seeks timelessness by associating death and its monuments with purity, beauty, and changelessness.

Thus, Twain loves Egypt because he sees it as an eternal land. In his hymn to the Sphinx, he celebrates it both for being eternal, "gazing out over the ocean of Time," and for being wise, sad, patient: "if ever image of stone thought, it was thinking." For Twain, the Sphinx endures forever in its memories and dreams amid the sands of a changing and illusory world (58).

Another type of the eternal for Twain is Damascus; he ends his narrative with it. Richard Bridgman observes that Twain presents a "severely idealized version" of the city and that he associates it with the Garden of Eden, Asian fables, and "unusual endurance." Bridgman argues that Twain ends with this image because "he wanted permanence, solidity, thereness."[18] Damascus, reputedly the oldest continuously inhabited city on earth, is, like the Sphinx, a point of stability amid flux. The Sphinx and especially Damascus, "the one city in all the world that has kept its name and held its place," suggest the possibility of a stable identity, something that Twain finds both appealing and threatening.

Twain implies a sense of fixity or the eternal in his discussions of human nature. For example, in his playful imaginary rendering of Roman Coliseum spectacles, Twain suggests that boys are boys, brash and irreverent no matter what the era, and that human behavior is relatively unchanging (26). Similarly, while musing among the lava-encrusted ruins of Pompeii, yet another city of the dead, he imagines a night at a Pompeiian theater in thoroughly modern terms (31). For Twain, this is one way to approach the problem of the past and to reconcile the past with the present: to imagine (often humorously) that the past is not so different from the present. The same motif expressed in his extolling of the Sphinx and Damascus is also expressed in his suggestion that there is a quality of the eternal in the human race, especially in its young people. Furthermore, by portraying the past in modern terms, he offers comic insights into human nature, showing that amusing human foibles haven't changed much over the centuries.

The strategies by which Twain seeks the eternal are many, but he seems to fear fixity as much as he longs for it. Cities of the dead are still just cemeteries; Damascus is a squalid and disheartening place. The eternal dream can become the eternal nightmare; fixity can become a trap. The legend of the Wandering Jew, which fascinates Twain, is also a type of the eternal, but of eternal suffering, eternal yearning for release, eternal rounds without goal or hope (54). The impoverished, unchanging little villages that he describes, from the Azores to Palestine, are also models of eternity—an eternity of squalor and ignorance.

Moreover, to give up change for stability is to give up the novelty that the creative mind relishes. At times Twain's discussion of eternity is relatively humorless; he tends to give up the comic sporting of attitudes that characterizes him at his best. It can be difficult to synthesize the wisdom of the eternal mind with the humor of the temporal observer.

There are other problems. Twain often has trouble ending his narratives; perhaps he fears the finality of form—it is a type of death.[19] Indeed, Twain suggests that he both longs for and fears a fixed identity for his narratives and himself; at the same time, he both wants and distrusts the volatility of humor. Change involves the perishable concrete, the horrors of mutability; but eternity involves abstraction, with the attendant dangers of sterility, self-imprisonment, and humorlessness. The abstract and the concrete, the eternal and the temporal, the past and the present, are not easily reconciled. One brilliance of *The Innocents Abroad* is that Twain is not afraid to confront such philosophical and psychological problems, even in the context of a comic narrative. He is not afraid to present the difficulties his humor must face.

Such problems influence Twain's development as persona, for he wants to be both stable and versatile, mindful of eternal abstractions yet alert to the ever-changing world around him. Twain tries to establish or identify himself as a comic personality who can handle problems posed by both the past and the present. As a result, he emerges as much more than a mere "humorist": he emerges as a variegated and thoughtful mind, cognizant of existential dilemmas but also cognizant that humor can shape new perspectives on these dilemmas. By shaping new perspectives, humor lets him shape a relatively free identity.

His continuing preoccupation with questions of identity is shown by his interest in Joseph, an Old Testament character frequently mentioned in Twain's writings. Betrayed by his own brothers, thrown into a pit, sold into slavery, yet able to become the most influential man in eternal Egypt, Joseph was beset by disorienting problems of identity similar to those Twain presents in *The Innocents Abroad*. Moreover, Joseph had a natural love of show (the coat of many colors), he was able to assert himself despite being in a foreign land, and he enjoyed playing roles and games, deceiving his brothers. Most important, Joseph was able to maintain a secure sense of who he was while adapting to a new land and a new life. Like Joseph, Twain tries to assert himself in a confusing, threatening world.

Twain notes that Joseph attained power over those (his brothers) who once had power over him: "they were trembling beggars—he, the lord of a mighty empire!" (47). Twain sometimes seems humiliated by the Old World and evinces a desire to gain power over it, to reverse his fortunes as Joseph did his. The power of the Old World and the existential problems he faces are threatening; in response, Twain tries to dispel these threats through comic narrative.

He is predominantly successful, for *The Innocents Abroad* vibrates with lively, imaginative humor. Twain revels in humor for its own sake; moreover, humor often seems for him what a poem is for Frost, "a momentary stay against confusion." It lets him create a personal order—or at least his *own* form of disorder—thereby presenting himself as his narrative's locus. Scholars such as James Cox, Bruce Michelson, and Warwick Wadlington have emphasized Twain's love of play, games, and the pleasure principle. Michelson, for instance, notes Twain's use of improvisation in *The Innocents Abroad* to convert touring into play; Wadlington celebrates the book's variety of perspectives, its plasticity, and Twain's assertion of himself.[20]

One way in which Twain uses humor is to try to reshape the world according to his imagination and wishes. For example, he is appalled to find his Parisian guide named "Billfinger" (an apt name actually, given his greed), so Twain renames him "Ferguson," which becomes Twain's standard name for all guides. Twain thus Americanizes his foreign guides, rendering them familiar and supposedly subject to control (13). Similarly, faced by a monotonous series of dreary Arab villages with unpronounceable names, he gives them place-names such as "Jacksonville" (42). Throughout his narrative, Twain tries to reconstruct the Old World according to his own terms, thus making himself, not the Old World, his narrative's dominant theme.

Twain also uses humor in an effort to limit the power of anything that threatens him. We've seen that he taunts guides. He and the doctor repeatedly ask guides, "Is he dead?" when discussing figures from long ago, thereby turning the dead past into humor (27). Faced with the nonsense and exaggerations of Europe, Twain responds with his own. When Russian nobles try to impress him with their grandeur, he responds with a tall tale about an uncle who fell down a mine shaft and broke himself in two. Confronted by Baron Ungern-Sternberg, director of Russian railroads, who employs almost ten thousand convicts, Twain rises to the occasion: "This appeared to be another call on my resources. I was equal to the emergency. I said we had eighty thousand convicts employed on the railways in America—all of them under sentence of death for murder in the first degree. That closed *him* out" (37).

Faced by the sheer abundance of artworks in the Old World, bewildered by the disorder he sees, Twain substitutes his own brand of creative confusion. He introduces a measured dose of anarchy by having his description of his ascent of Vesuvius constantly interrupted by rambling digressions. Consequently, five or six sections entitled "Ascent of Vesuvius Continued" occur before "The Summit Reached" (29–30). Twain makes his narrative mirror the disorder of the world, with his own humorous polish added.

He adopts a similar tactic with legends that he knows to be absurd but cannot actually disprove. Shown the alleged tomb of Adam in the Church of the Holy Sepulchre, Twain weeps ludicrously over the grave. He mourns, "Noble old man—he did not live to see me—he did not live to see his child. And I—I—alas, I did not live to see *him"* (53). In such wildly illogical lines Twain simultaneously celebrates and attacks human irrationality; he suggests that humor and absurdity are closely related, depending on the blurring of conventional categories of thought (in this case, distinctions based on chronology). He removes some of the heavy burden of human irrationality and substitutes some light nonsense of his own—nonsense not weighted down by superstition, tradition, and antiquity. Like St. Helena, alleged discoverer of the True Cross, he starts "finding" his own artifacts; he creates his own "legends."

Elsewhere Twain humorously mocks superstition, claiming alleged miracles *must* have occurred because he has seen the place of their occurrence. At other times he disregards the implausibility of various myths and adapts them to his own creative purposes, as when he uses the Ephesian "Legend of the Seven Sleepers" to insert humorous dialect, poke fun at the shady characters of the seven sleepers, and implicitly raise questions about time and identity (40). Indeed, Twain never hesitates to treat a legend as factual if it lets him create humor or make a telling point about human nature; in later writings he uses the stories of Adam and Noah, among others. By altering myths for his own humorous ends, Twain again makes himself the narrative's center: he controls how we think and feel about these myths.

In response to the Old World's wish to impress him with its spectacles, Twain creates spectacles of his own. His re-creation of the ancient world in his passages on the Roman Coliseum and Pompeii demonstrate Twain's comic virtuosity and ability to create effects. Thus, in the Coliseum episode, Twain pretends to discover an ancient playbill and imaginatively repopulates the Coliseum with gladiators, barbarians, ferocious wild animals, spectators (including dandies, fine young ladies, and insolent little boys), and journalists. He even presents a review of the day's fights from the *Roman Daily Battle-Ax*. Twain also presents tragedy: the grief of those who lose loved ones in the arena is poignantly shown. He satirizes both the mindless cruelty of the contests and the inanity of journalists (26). By mingling such elements with humor, he is developing an approach that lets him present the many-sidedness of experience—a multiplicity that has been impressed upon him by the various existential challenges surveyed elsewhere in his narrative. The arena of life presents many simultaneous acts; what one sees depends on where one looks.

All of these humorous techniques let Twain reduce the Old World's power over him. He recognizes the customary historical associations of, say, the Coliseum, yet he also creates his own associations for it. In other words, Twain does not let the Old World and its past dictate to him just what associations of thought and emotion he will have. He thereby avoids fixity. His comic play helps him fashion new links; he is free to grow and think in ways not determined by the Old World. Confronted by the watery but dilapidated grandeur of Venice, Twain conjures up the image of a flooded Arkansas river town (22); traveling by French railway car leads him to recall "the infinitely more delightful" experience of traveling by stagecoach in the American West (12); and the Phidian statue with the "skinned alive" look moves him to tell an anecdote about a boyhood encounter with a corpse: "I went away from there . . . I went out at the window, and I carried the sash along with me. I did not need the sash, but it was handier to take it than it was to leave it, and so I took it" (18). Perhaps most unexpectedly, the mysterious veins of oyster shells in the hills of Smyrna prompt him to recollect quartz mining in Nevada Territory and to consider locating a "claim" on these oyster veins: "We, the undersigned, claim five claims of two hundred feet each, (and one for discovery,) on this ledge or lode of oyster-shells, with all its dips, spurs, angles, variations and sinuosities, and fifty feet on each side of the same, to work it, etc., etc., according to the mining laws of Smyrna" (39). Again and again, seemingly almost effortlessly, Twain gives his sightseeing experiences new dimensions.

His humor also lets Twain present himself as relatively invulnerable to various Old World threats. One method is the hoax. Although Twain doesn't revel in hoaxes in this narrative to the extent that he does in his western journalism, he enjoys exerting his power through occasional duplicity. He targets not only the Old World but also his readers. Mark Twain presents mixed attitudes toward his audience, perhaps arising from Samuel Clemens's fears of being perceived as a beggar or buffoon. Moreover, because Clemens made his excursion largely for the sake of the reading public, his ambivalent feelings about the trip may be reflected in Twain's stance toward the reader. In any case, Twain seems to strive to bring both the Old World and his readers under control.

In his hilarious account of his sufferings at the hands of a Parisian barber (12), Twain at first appears to be poking fun only at himself for his gullibility—a standard Twain pose, but also a standard Twain way of gulling (and disarming) his readers. Upon reflection, we realize Twain is lampooning French pretensions to luxury and refinement, and upon further reflection we realize he is doing so at our expense, playing upon our credulity. Indeed, Twain has given us another tall tale, replete with exaggerations of violence and suffering; if we are foolish enough to believe that French barbers really shave people this way, so much the worse for us. With one swoop Twain nicks both the French and his American readers.

Similarly, he poses as a naïf when smoking a Turkish narghile pipe: "I exploded one mighty cough, and it was as if Vesuvius had let go." He complains, "When I think how I have been swindled by books of Oriental travel, I want a tourist for breakfast" (34). But though Twain suggests that Turkish luxury is as fraudulent as French luxury, it is the reader who has once again been swindled. If we believe that Twain is really smoking "at every pore, like a frame house that is on fire on the inside," then it is we, not Twain, who are enveloped in smoke. Not long afterward we find Twain reclining on a divan in Damascus, contentedly smoking a narghile (44).

Twain presents such anecdotes in part as entertainment, but he also gains power, control, and, most important, originality. One is supposed to *enjoy* French shaves and Turkish pipes, but Twain delights in the unexpected, the different. Indeed, much of his humor is designed to discover something new, even if it demolishes the conventional dream of pleasure. Shortly before his playful invention of the Coliseum playbill, Twain says, "What is it that confers the noblest delight? What is that which swells a man's breast with pride above that which any other experience can bring to him? Discovery!" He adds, "To be the first—that is the idea" (26). He laments that there is nothing new in Rome to discover, which is why he has to *invent* the Coliseum of the playbill. Similarly, he fears *The Last Supper* as an aesthetic standard, an absolute that cannot be changed or surpassed: "The world seems to have become settled in the belief, long ago, that it is not possible for human genius to outdo this creation of Da Vinci's. I suppose painters will go on copying it as long as any of the original is left visible to the eye" (19). Twain may fear that the Old World's standards and his readers' expectations will circumscribe him, reduce him to the status of mere copyist. He uses humor to upset those standards and expectations, to create new perspectives, to begin to create his world and himself anew. Near narrative's end he has sufficient confidence in his powers to invent "notebook" entries (59).[21]

He is also not afraid to conjoin words or ideas in unexpected, comic ways, as when he notes, "The gentle reader will never, never know what a consummate ass he can become, until he goes abroad" (23). The biblical reference to the "voice of the turtle" prompts Twain to imagine a fellow tourist so ignorant that he sits for an hour in the blistering sun of Palestine waiting for a mud turtle to sing (47). And Twain constantly invents "facts," speculations, and theories. Impressed by the vastness and vagueness of history, and by the limitations of historical knowledge, he imagines an encyclopedic entry for Ulysses S. Grant forty centuries hence, in which Grant ("Uriah S. [or Z.] Graunt") is described as a "popular poet of ancient times in the Aztec provinces of the United States of British America. . . . He wrote 'Rock me to Sleep, Mother'" (31). For those who wonder what becomes of all the Egyptian mummies, Twain has a ready explanation: they are burned as railroad locomotive fuel, "purchased by the ton or by the graveyard for that purpose . . . sometimes one hears the profane engineer call out pettishly, 'D—n these plebeians, they don't burn worth a cent—pass out a King'" (58). And as for those enigmatic oyster veins high in the Smyrnan hills—the veins Twain wants to mine—he has his theory, "slender" though he admits it to be, as to how they got there:

The oysters climbed up there of their own accord. But what object could they have had in view—what did they want up there? . . . To climb a hill must necessarily be fatiguing and annoying exercise for an oyster. The most natural conclusion would be that the oysters climbed up there to look at the scenery. Yet when one comes to reflect upon the nature of an oyster, it seems plain that he does not care for scenery. . . . An oyster is of a retiring disposition, and not lively—not even cheerful above the average, and never enterprising. (39)

Thus forced by hard logic to discard his theory, Twain admits that he is left with the simple fact that the oyster shells are there and that nobody knows how they got there. But it is Twain's hilarious theorizing that we are most likely to remember; throughout much of *The Innocents Abroad* it is his mind—his comic imaginings, memories, and speculations—that impresses us the most.

When the world is too much with him, when the dead past bears down too heavily upon him, Mark Twain sometimes counters by substituting a creative version of Samuel Clemens's past, which thus becomes Mark Twain's "past." By supplanting the Old World's past with his own past, Twain has another way to make himself the narrative's central theme. He makes lively mention of his western adventures, and he presents anecdotes about an ordeal at the Benton House and a boyhood exploit on Holliday's Hill. In the Benton House story, Twain describes a hotel as bad as or worse than the worst Old World hotel: "We are stopping at Shepherd's Hotel [Cairo], which is the worst on earth except the one I stopped at once in a small town in the United States. . . . I can stand Shepherd's Hotel sure, because I have been in one just like it in America and survived." Twain then tells his hotel horror tale. "The Benton is not a good hotel. The Benton lacks a very great deal of being a good hotel. Perdition is full of better hotels than the Benton" (57). Shabby furniture, inadequate lighting, a crusty old landlord, a lying but accommodating porter, and a general lack of amenities round out Twain's picture of the Benton. Twain demonstrates that no matter what trials the Old World inflicts upon him, he is equal to the challenge: he will laughingly tell of greater discomforts endured, drawing on his "past" and humorous resources.

In the Holliday's Hill story, Twain relates a boyhood triumph: he and a friend, after much digging, managed to start a huge boulder from its place. "It was splendid. It went crashing down the hillside, tearing up saplings, mowing bushes down like grass, ripping and crushing and smashing everything in its path" (58). Twain may not always be able to budge the Old World, but he can take amusing consolation in his narrative of an obstacle he did overcome. The boulder's wild, glorious momentum symbolizes Twain at his bounding best; he seems to wish he could smash the Old World's shams the way the boulder smashed "everything in its path."

Both anecdotes are fresher and funnier than the Old World accounts in which they are embedded. On such occasions Mark Twain presents not the Old World but Mark Twain regenerating himself through embellished accounts of Samuel Clemens's experiences. His presentation of himself as his narrative's controlling theme gives a locus for his varied responses. His modulated, humorous voice shapes the reader's perceptions and prevents the narrative from disintegrating into helplessness or chaos. To a large extent, Twain's comic narrative lets him reshape both his world and himself.

Through his diverse strategies of humor and his consideration not only of the Old World but also of many aspects and dilemmas of life generally, Twain emerges as a kaleidoscopic, thoughtful, inclusive presence. Outraged by tourists' relic-hunting, Twain nevertheless can invent a scene of remarkably light comedy: at Sevastopol, "Blucher" improvises by labeling the jawbone of a horse "Fragment of a Russian General" (35). Condemning much of Catholicism, Twain nevertheless can acknowledge "the charity, the purity, the unselfishness" of Dominican friars who risk their lives tending the ill during a cholera epidemic in Naples (25). Constantly decrying illusion based on distance (whether in space or time), Twain nevertheless can recognize the importance of such perspectives, whether it be an "enchanted memory" of boyhood or of Jerusalem, or a distant view of St. Peter's grandly swelling above Rome (54, 55). "When one is traveling in Europe, the daily incidents seem all alike; but when he has placed them all two months and two thousand miles behind him, those that were worthy of being remembered are prominent, and those that were really insignificant have vanished" (55). And perhaps most wonderful of all, while lampooning the buffoonery all around him, Twain nevertheless can easily present himself as a buffoon at times, as when he is deluded by a shop girl's praises (and his own vanity) into buying shabby kid gloves (7), or when he asserts that the ship's coffee is inferior—only to learn that it is tea: "The humbled mutineer smelt it, tasted it, and returned to his seat. He had made an egregious ass of himself before the whole ship. He did it no more. After that he took things as they came. That was me" (60). In short, Twain gains variety, perspective, and humanness. His masterful narrative voice can laugh at the world—or at itself. And though Twain never really takes things as they come—much to our delight, he constantly rearranges, exaggerates, invents—he nevertheless is always before us, *there,* whether in his views of the Old World or in his memories of his "past." He might say of *The Innocents Abroad:* "That was me." And, notwithstanding occasional confusions and difficulties in development, "me" is remarkably imaginative, interesting, and diverse—a literary personality to be reckoned with, potent in humor.

Some limits do remain, of course. When the Old World pressures him too heavily, Twain doesn't always have at hand an amusing anecdote about his past—and other humorous techniques sometimes fail. For example, renaming people and places may not help much, for names bounce off things: Billfinger remains mercenary after being rechristened "Ferguson"; Arab villages remain dirty and squalid after being given American place-names. Indeed, sometimes humor ricochets off a recalcitrant reality. At times, the playful exaggerations and Twain grow tired while life's trials remain; the vast, brooding presence of the Old World remains, too often impervious to creative reshaping. Twain notes of Ephesus:

> It makes me feel as old as these dreary hills to look down upon these moss-hung ruins, this historic desolation. One may read the Scriptures and believe, but he can not go and stand yonder in the ruined theatre and in imagination people it again with the vanished multitudes who mobbed Paul's comrades there and shouted, with one voice, "Great is Diana of the Ephesians!" The idea of a shout in such a solitude as this almost makes one shudder. (40)

Parts of *The Innocents Abroad* display Twain shouting in solitude, trying to recover a lost past, a lost religious perspective, a lost cultural context, a lost self. He can comically repopulate the Roman Coliseum; he cannot repopulate the Ephesian amphitheater.

One returns to the Sphinx, which, like so much of the Old World, simply remains. Like Twain, the Sphinx finds itself alone in a desolate solitude, "the stony dreamer solitary" in a world it knows not, trying to recover the past. Twain emblematizes it as "MEMORY":

> After years of waiting, it was before me at last. The great face was so sad, so earnest, so longing, so patient. There was a dignity not of earth in its mien, and in its countenance a benignity such as never any thing human wore. It was stone, but it seemed sentient. If ever image of stone thought, it was thinking. It was looking toward the verge of the landscape, yet looking *at* nothing—nothing but distance and vacancy. It was looking over and beyond everything of the present, and far into the past. It was gazing out over the ocean of Time. (58)

Twain has given the Sphinx his own narrative preoccupations: this tribute to cosmic memory comes immediately after his narration of Samuel Clemens's boyhood prank on Holliday's Hill. One senses that Twain, like the Sphinx, aspires to the cosmic, to rise above the incongruities, problems of the past, and quandaries of identity that his narrative faces. Yet Twain wishes not to lapse into the Sphinx's fixity—abstract, austere, remote. Despite the triumphs of *The Innocents Abroad,* Twain as yet has offered no final, comprehensive solution; the problems, like the Sphinx, remain. But if the Sphinx has patience, Twain has humor. Perhaps the comic can become the cosmic. His works after *The Innocents Abroad* reveal what Twain sees when he, too, looks out over the "ocean of Time."

4

⚭

Open Range

Persona and Humor in *Roughing It*

As he nears the end of *The Innocents Abroad,* Mark Twain sometimes seems tired and discouraged. His satirical letter to the *New
York Herald,* intended to make the pilgrims "get up and howl," at
times lapses into grumbling about a shipboard life of "solemnity,
decorum, dinner, dominoes, devotions, slander." Given Samuel Clemens's previous travels, Mark Twain prevaricates when he says:
"None of us had ever been anywhere before." If he had added that
he had not yet completely succeeded in transforming the experiences of Clemens into the comic adventures of Twain, he would
have been telling the truth, mainly, about both his western journalism and *The Innocents Abroad.* While successful in many ways,
these narratives present a Mark Twain who is still trying to find
ways to evolve as a persona and to shape experience.

In *Roughing It*—which was published in 1872, three years after
The Innocents Abroad—Twain discovers for the first time how to
control a comic narrative fully, with humor relocating reality into
consciousness.[1] In other words, "reality" now becomes what Twain
says it is; in *Roughing It* he controls experience and the world.
Moreover, the relatively new and unformed West, unlike the fixed,
culture-laden Old World, often lends itself to fabrication and fantasy, letting Twain become more fluid (yet masterful) than ever before. Through humor Twain molds the West into *his* world; he uses
events rather than being used by them. He revels in the West's incongruities and ironies, confident in his ability to convert confusion

into game—or at least into *amusing* confusion. Incongruities become enjoyable ironies; Twain holds linguistic sway over the adventures he narrates. By surveying a given event from diverse perspectives and shaping it through comic narration, Twain is free and in control; his best humor arises when he can simultaneously present life's quandaries and suggest invulnerability to them. Often it is as though Twain winks to the reader, implying, "I can exaggerate or invent at will; incongruities and frustrations are but playful challenges; no matter what stressful events I narrate, my narrative voice is in control." The experiences of Samuel Clemens become the fiction of Mark Twain.

Although the preface declares that "this book is merely a personal narrative," *Roughing It* is not so much an account of Samuel Clemens's western experiences as it is Mark Twain's fantasy, play, and speculation. Clemens's memory of his actual experiences was sometimes so dim that he had to ask his brother Orion for notes on their overland stagecoach journey, as well as borrow from travel books. One senses throughout *Roughing It* that Clemens's western experiences, though they may at times illuminate the West of the 1860s, actually serve as the pretext for Twain's humor and development. We see the West that Twain wants us to see: the West of his imagination and comic language. As Lee Clark Mitchell notes, the West of Twain's narrative is not so much a place as an "angle of vision."[2]

Indeed, *Roughing It* is really about Twain, not about the West. Twain's preface may add that "there is quite a good deal of information in the book," information that "stews out" of him like the "precious ottar of roses out of the otter." This information, however, is mostly about the source from which it leaks. The book's "variegated vagabondizing" is a trip through the theater of Twain's comic roles and perspectives.

Such a trip is hardly linear. Like *The Innocents Abroad, Roughing It* lacks a straightforward narrative structure with one episode building naturally upon another. Like the Mississippi River, Twain swirls, eddies, and makes horseshoe bends; but it is this free flow of humor that makes his book successful. Most critics who talk about structure in *Roughing It* focus on Twain's supposed transformation from tenderfoot to old-timer—a simplistic pattern that does not do justice to Twain's complex narrative.

There *is* a pattern of sorts to *Roughing It:* a pattern of humorous transcendence, expressed through the interplay of anecdotes and perspectives in the narrative. Through such innovative interplay Twain expands as a persona, as a medley of voices and views; he shapes and controls the protean world he manufactures for us. Twain's anecdotes relate to one another—and to his narrative as a whole—not in a fixed structure but in seemingly innumerable and variable ways, giving us a narrative that is as flexible as its narrator. Twain's anecdotes illuminate one another. For instance, not until readers reach the anecdote about the Admiral and Williams manufacturing "history" (62) are they likely to realize to what extent Twain is inventing history throughout his narrative. Indeed, readers may find themselves reconsidering previous anecdotes. The Washoe Zephyr anecdote (21) suggests that such gradations of "fact" and blurring of distinctions may recondition the way the reader views earlier anecdotes such as Bemis's buffalo tale or the story about Eckert's coconut-eating cat. In turn, these anecdotes help anticipate, for example, the anecdote about the great landslide case, in which the very earth of reality seems to shake and move.

Twain uses this interplay to derive a transcendent perspective. As such, the movement of the book is not forward but upward, through diverse levels of comic play and creation. Twain reacts to the challenges and shocks of the unfettered West by surmounting its divisions, extremes, and polarities. He celebrates the West's openness: a man may play many roles; the West offers many opportunities for linguistic games. Free to remake word and world, Twain suggests at yet a higher plane that he is thereby free to reinvent narrative structure, history, and even truth. Such reinvention may in turn lead to the remaking of one's very conceptions of "reality" and "identity," suggesting that both may be continually recast in the creative mind. Such continual creation becomes re-creation (or sophisticated recreation), comic sporting that allows Twain to shape the West and his narrative. Such play offers both solutions and problems.

Twain experimented with various forms of expression in articles written before and during the writing of *Roughing It.* In his "Memoranda" columns for the *Galaxy*, which he wrote from 1868 to 1871, he shows his understanding of human nature, extends his use of hoaxes and exaggerations, plays with perspective, and adopts multiple roles. His writings celebrate imagination's power over reality. He notes about his friend and fellow writer John Henry Riley: "I would rather have one chatty paragraph of his fancy than a whole obituary of his facts."[3] In various sketches Twain suggests it is not the object but the subject, the perceiver-creator, that matters. Perspective determines what is seen. In his 1870 piece "My Watch: An Instructive Little Tale," Twain presents a funny medley of views on how to fix his watch, each opinion dependent on the background of the particular watchmaker involved. Thus, the last watchmaker, a former steamboat engineer, opines, "She makes too much steam—you want to hang the monkey-wrench on the safety-valve." Twain notes, "I brained him on the spot, and had him buried at my own expense."[4] Despite the title, the tale's subject is not Twain's watch (which never gets fixed), but rather the delightful discord of cock-eyed opinions offered by assorted watchmakers.

In his *Galaxy* contributions Twain presents himself in a wide range of roles: a wise simpleton in "How I Edited an Agricultural Paper"; a pretentious, single-minded idiot in "Political Economy"; and a brash ignoramus, the self-important westerner at his worst, in "The Reception at the President's." In such articles it is not the ostensible topic that matters, but the "I"—madcap, multifaceted Mark Twain. He moves easily from role to role, with more mobility than in his previous writings; he offers more aspects or images of himself. Although Twain still tends to limit himself to a given role in a given piece, the role is often more versatile than previous roles. For instance, while he plays the fool in much of "How I Edited an Agricultural Paper," at the end he brilliantly lampoons editors (and the human race generally) for their conceit in pretending to know more than they do. A complex picture of Twain emerges from just this one piece.

Throughout these articles Twain is developing a theatrics of the soul, a dramatized love of imaginative lies. He closes his series of "Memoranda" columns with an anecdote about a man named Markiss, who is such a consummate liar that when he kills himself the jury refuses to believe that he committed suicide or that he is even dead. In this tall tale, which is included in the Sandwich Islands section of *Roughing It,* Twain portrays himself as the victim of Markiss, always being out-lied by the master liar; the encompassing joke is that Mark Twain has created Markiss, has lied him into existence and has induced us to believe in him. Mark is Markiss. It is Twain who is the supreme liar, or rather, the master fictionist: he blurs distinctions between fact and fiction, logic and absurdity, death and life. In *Roughing It* he dissolves many distinctions, categories, and conventions.

As in his earlier western writings, Twain presents the West as a world apart, in conflict with the East; but in *Roughing It,* instead of seeming confused by such conflict, Twain offers vivid, brilliantly funny images of the West. He asserts control through a series of humorous vignettes; he uses the West to generate images that he then appropriates to increase his power and versatility. For example, in his anecdote about a coyote and a town-dog, Twain suggests the power of the cunning, deceitful West over the naïve, self-satisfied East:

> But if you start a swift-footed dog after him [the coyote], you will enjoy it ever so much—especially if it is a dog that has a good opinion of himself, and has been brought up to think he knows something about speed. The cayote [*sic*] will go swinging gently off on that deceitful trot of his, and every little while he will smile a fraudful smile over his shoulder that will fill that dog entirely full of encouragement and worldly ambition, and make him lay his head still lower to the ground, and stretch his neck further to the front, and pant more fiercely, and stick his tail out straighter behind, and move his furious legs with a yet wilder frenzy, and leave a broader and broader, and higher and denser cloud of desert sand smoking behind, and marking his long wake across the level plain! And all this time the dog is only a short twenty feet behind the cayote, and to save the soul of him he cannot understand why it is that he cannot get perceptibly closer; and he begins to get aggravated, and it makes him madder and madder to see how gently the cayote glides along and never pants or sweats or ceases to smile; and he grows still more and more incensed to see how shamefully he has been taken in by an entire stranger, and what an ignoble swindle that long, calm, soft-footed trot is; and next he notices that he is getting fagged, and that the cayote actually has to slacken speed a little to keep from running away from him—and *then* that town-dog is mad in earnest, and he begins to strain and weep and swear, and paw the sand higher than ever, and reach for

the cayote with concentrated and desperate energy. This "spurt" finds him six feet behind the gliding enemy, and two miles from his friends. And then, in the instant that a wild new hope is lighting up his face, the cayote turns and smiles blandly upon him once more, and with a something about it which seems to say: "Well, I shall have to tear myself away from you, bub—business is business, and it will not do for me to be fooling along this way all day"—and forthwith there is a rushing sound, and the sudden splitting of a long crack through the atmosphere, and behold that dog is solitary and alone in the midst of a vast solitude! (5)

The tale anticipates Twain's story of himself in the West: he seeks the wealth the West seems to promise, only to find it forever receding from him. More important, the story reflects the experience of many of the book's readers: they expect to run meaning to earth, to seize upon sense at last, only to find empty air. Eastern literary expectations are left frustrated in the midst of a desert of absurdity.

In his narrative Twain retreats before the reader, just as the coyote does before the town-dog. The reader is rarely sure what a passage *means*. In this instance, is the coyote a hero or a villain? Are we to pity or scorn the deluded town-dog? The coyote is among the fastest of canines, but can we believe he is as fast as Twain says? Having transmuted the trickery of the West into his own trickery, Twain leaves his readers laughing—and guessing. Whatever town-dog humiliations of his own Twain may narrate, he has now appropriated the image of the coyote for himself, thereby suggesting that he controls his narrative and his readers. The coyote is not, however, presented as fat and contented: "The cayote [*sic*] is a long, slim, sick and sorry-looking skeleton, with a gray wolf-skin stretched over it, a tolerably bushy tail that forever sags down with a despairing expression of forsakenness and misery, a furtive and evil eye, and a long, sharp face, with slightly lifted lip and exposed teeth. He has a general slinking expression all over. The cayote is a living, breathing allegory of Want." To the extent that he makes the coyote's image his own, Twain indicates the ravages he undergoes in the West. Impoverished in San Francisco, he describes himself as "slinking," mean, and low (59). Yet Twain relates the coyote anecdote—and most of his narrative—with relish. He is as "cheerful" as the Allen revolver, which never hits what it is aimed at but always manages to "fetch" something else instead (2). Although *Roughing It* shows Twain's failure to become rich, it also shows his success in producing an imaginative treatment of the West and converting pain into pleasure. The coyote achieves transcendence through fleetness of foot; Twain achieves transcendence through fleetness of narration.

Twain needs all the narrative fleetness and agility he can command in the West, for it is a land of extremes, of contrasts to the East, and of subversions of conventions. The West's dialects, customs, and clothes are presented in the early chapters as humorous shocks to Twain's system. The voyage into Twain's West is a voyage across the divide between sanity and madness, or the divide between this world and the next. Deserts are presented as bizarre dreamscapes of beauty and death; Mormons are presented as alien creatures with unfathomable customs; and outlaws such as Slade are presented as puzzling mixtures of barbarism and refinement. Fascinated by the Continental Divide, where one stream flows all the way to the Atlantic while a neighboring stream finds its way to the Pacific, Twain faces a rugged land that constantly tends to polarize existence, to make life a series of incomprehensible oppositions (12). A land free of the laws of men yet possessed of a higher law, violent and childlike, deceitful and open, the vast West is simultaneously nothingness and infinite possibility. Twain strives not to be torn apart by such polarities or reduced to the dualisms and set perspectives that too often plague his earlier narratives. He seeks to control the West's binary oppositions and imaginatively fill the void left by the destruction of conventional expectations. He fills the void with himself.

The task is difficult, though, and there are some tendencies toward dualities in *Roughing It*. For instance, Twain elaborates upon the greed of westerners, yet he sets in sharp opposition an exaggerated account of western generosity in his tale of the Sanitary Flour Sack Fund (45).[5] Similarly, he exaggerates shifts of fortune, both good and bad, often showing himself as the victim of chance. Struck by such contrary winds blowing at times through the book, Kolb declares that Twain "pursues oppositions relentlessly."[6] Kolb overstates the case, but it is true that Twain sometimes succumbs to his former tendency to view human nature or the world in stark, divisive terms: human beings are saints or devils; the West enriches or impoverishes. As in his earlier writings, whenever Twain oscillates between such polarities, he seems to countenance only simplistic, black-and-white notions of morality, truth, and fortune. The nuances of life are lost.

As a result, despite the narrative's general exuberance and the complex play of Twain's humor at its best, *Roughing It* is frequently read as a book of pat dualities and disappointments. For instance, in *The Pattern for Mark Twain's "Roughing It,"* Rogers argues that Twain has dual roles of tenderfoot and old-timer. According to Rogers, the narrative relates the initiation of a tenderfoot into the ways of the West, showing how he becomes a sophisticated, realistic (if not cynical) old-timer. Everett Emerson also views *Roughing It* as an initiation experience but considers the Sandwich Islands section weak because the theme of initiation is lost. Finally, Smith asserts that Twain's initiation ends with the snowstorm scene in which Twain is lost but survives and is supposedly "reborn" into the West. Smith agrees with Rogers about Twain's dual roles but adds that both are present in the narrative from the start. He points out that it is old-timer Twain who is presenting the whole narrative, his voice inevitably blending with the views of tenderfoot Twain, even in the early sections.[7]

Such readings have dominated critical discussion of *Roughing It*. While the initiation theme is certainly important to the narrative, to stress it oversimplifies both the narrative's approach to the West (and experience generally) and Twain's evolving persona. It ignores the extent to which the entire work, including the Sandwich Islands section, develops a complex array of perspectives. *Roughing It* suggests that the ambiguities of life are often not reducible to polarities. Furthermore, Twain implies that the mind shapes and manufactures "experience" and that consciousness is fluid—again, motifs that cannot be reduced to polarities or fixed perspectives. His humor, whether expressed as hoaxes, tall tales, subtle deceptions, or seemingly innumerable mental games and traps, celebrates the mind's facility for changing ideas and contexts. The initiation experience in *Roughing It* never ends, for it is an initiation not so much into the ways of the West as into the ways the mind fashions and changes images of everything, including ourselves. Far from dividing into a simple duality, Twain keeps altering before our eyes.

Another problem with the classic dualism of tenderfoot and old-timer is that it implies one can come to know fully and objectively a given "reality," in this case the West. It suggests that the old-timer has "factual" knowledge that the tenderfoot does not have. But the mind is given to making illusions and reconstructing experience regardless of whether one is a tenderfoot or an old-timer. The old-timer may dream better dreams; the maker of *Roughing It* dreams a more sophisticated dream than the naïve youth filling his pockets with mica on a western hillside in the belief that he has found gold. The joy of adventure and discovery is present in both cases; both are manufacturing something out of nothing. The youth with his mica gains a few hours of believing that he is rich; the maker and reader of *Roughing It* gain a humorous—and insightful—narrative.

Twain not only presents himself as both tenderfoot and old-timer but also blends these stances until the opposition vanishes. For example, both tenderfoot and old-timer cherish freedom: "Even at this day it thrills me through and through to think of the life, the gladness and the wild sense of freedom that used to make the blood dance in my veins on those fine overland mornings!" (5). Many of the old-timer's anecdotes, such as his tale of the camel that swallowed too much, are as fanciful as the imaginings of the tenderfoot youth (3). Twain often presents himself as a naïve youth for humorous effect—but naïveté can be a form of wisdom, too. Twain tells the story of a youth named Jack, who believes that an overland stage agent renowned for efficiency could have gotten the Israelites through the desert in thirty-six hours, instead of the forty years it took Moses. Here Twain presents an image of himself as an innocent going through the deserts of the West: ignorant, but with a touchstone for detecting popular illusions (6). Tenderfoot and old-timer alike delight in the joy of discovery and are equally adept at uncovering our illusions and vanities. As a tenderfoot, Twain may be suckered into buying a Mexican Plug, but soon he has many people, including old-timers, going out for a ride on the bucking horse, and coming back on foot (24). Tenderfoot Twain may have his pockets full of worthless mica, but for a time he even has old-timer Ballou excited, believing that perhaps gold nuggets *are* lying on the hillsides (28). Tenderfoot and old-timer are but phases of the same personality. When Twain asserts, after listening to Johnson's tales about Brigham Young's polygamous life, that "some instinct or other made me set this Johnson down as being unreliable," it is difficult to know whether tenderfoot Twain or old-timer Twain is talking (15).

Indeed, to call Twain a tenderfoot or an old-timer is to do an injustice to his complicated nature. Distinctions belie fluidity. Twain may sometimes rely upon such polarities, especially in the early chapters; moreover, the extremes of the West at times may induce Twain into dualities. But his humor generally depends on gradations, continua, and the fluidity of himself as persona. In *Roughing It,* Twain undercuts conventions and categories; he develops a play of comic attitudes that carries him, with increasing sophistication, not only through this narrative but through many later ones as well.

Twain faces difficulties in controlling the material of the West because it is so confusing and illusory. Distances are deceptive, with mountains appearing much closer than they are; the climate is bewildering, with snow in the mountains in July; the deserts have the incongruities of dreams; and the American Indians are nothing like the "noble savages" Twain expects from Cooper's writings. People pursue phantoms such as the long-lost Whiteman cement mine, and mining speculation leads to insane delusions. As we saw in Twain's journalism, even newspaper reporting is subject to vagaries and fanciful exaggerations, such as the puffing of mining stock. When Twain describes how he and two companions become lost in a snowstorm, circling in their tracks and finally giving up in a sea of whiteness while a stagecoach station stands invisible only a few yards away, he presents a metaphor for the mystery of the West (31–33). In this blank new world, this cultural and epistemological void, there are no guideposts by which to know where one is and what is real. If one relies upon his past, tries to orient himself by the tracks of where he has been, he will be lost. In the ghostly West, once-booming mining towns waver and "pass away like a dream," while the few remaining miners are specters, dream figures without life or zest (60).

In such a land it seems impossible to *know* anything; hence, a man commonly will "back his judgment" not with reason but with a gun (9). Twain describes a typical western debate: "Then he rode over and began to rebuke the stranger with a six-shooter, and the stranger began to explain with another" (21). Granted, words flow easily in the West; every wildcat miner is eager to inform everyone about his latest claim. Twain notes as he ponders the "Mormon question" upon leaving Salt Lake City: "We had a deal more 'information' than we had before, of course, but we did not know what portion of it was reliable and what was not" (17).

Such ambiguity allows considerable freedom, freedom offering both opportunity and threat. For Twain, the West is still open range, not yet fenced in by the barbed wire of facts; but it is possible to become lost on that open range, too. When Twain gives us statistics on mining production, when he gives what facts he *does* have, he is driving some fence posts and stringing some wire (36, 52), for without some enclosure there can be no real narrative freedom. Indeed, in a land where there is so little fact and so much illusion, there is ironically the constant danger of *disillusionment,* of abandoning oneself to ignorance, isolation, and despair. Henry Nash Smith, Hamlin Hill, and Tom Towers have noted a strain of disillusionment in *Roughing It.* Smith's observations on the mountain man, cut off from civilization and knowledge, apply at times to Twain: "[The lonely western life] throws the hero back in upon himself and accentuates his terrible and sublime isolation. He is an anarchic and self-contained atom—hardly even a monad—alone in a hostile, or at best a neutral, universe."[8] Dreams of discovery and wealth dissipate in the measureless openness of the West; Twain must be careful that his own beliefs do not likewise dissipate.

The threat of collapse into chaos or despair is always present. In *Land of Savagery, Land of Promise,* Ray Allen Billington notes the West's threat to one's identity: "Typical was a German traveler who was gripped by a terrible sense of horror, of foreboding, as he made his solitary way across the vast plain: 'I felt my connection with the past was broken—the first symptom of various kinds of madness—when the meaning of life becomes so tragic that there was no rescue.'"[9] We've seen how the town-dog's self-image, its sense of identity, is destroyed. Twain presents the West's dangers, but he also indicates the opportunities for role-playing and self-expansion that the West offers. He opens *Roughing It* with a review of all the roles Orion is expected to assume: "My brother had just been appointed Secretary of Nevada Territory—an office of such majesty that it concentrated in itself the duties and dignities of Treasurer, Comptroller, Secretary of State, and Acting Governor in the Governor's absence." Twain expects Orion to have adventures enough for many men:

> Pretty soon he would be hundreds and hundreds of miles away on the great plains and deserts, and among the mountains of the Far West, and would see buffaloes and Indians, and prairie dogs, and antelopes, and have all kinds of adventures, and maybe get hanged or scalped, and have ever such a fine time, and write home and tell us all about it, and be a hero. And he would see the gold mines and the silver mines, and maybe go about of an afternoon when his work was done, and pick up two or three pailfuls of shining slugs, and nuggets of gold and silver on the hillside. And by and by he would become very rich, and return home by sea, and be able to talk as calmly about San Francisco and the ocean, and "the Isthmus" as if it was nothing of any consequence to have seen those marvels face to face. (1)

Such passages are often taken to signify Twain's youthful enthusiasm and innocence—and rightly so. Yet they also signify a West of the mind, a theater where one can experiment safely with different roles and perspectives. In the imaginary West of *Roughing It,* death can be just another mirage. One senses that Orion *could* "get hanged or scalped" and nonetheless "have ever such a fine time" and rise from his literary grave to tell us all about it. Even in the snowstorm scene, when Twain faces death by freezing, there is an enchanting unreality to it all: "A delicious dreaminess wrought its web about my yielding senses, while the snow-flakes wove a winding sheet about my conquered body. Oblivion came. The battle of life was done" (32). Of course, freezing induces drowsiness, but this passage evokes a dream sense that renders death harmless, unreal. Twain's narrative voice implicitly reassures us that life has not ended.

In a world where the self is not limited or definite, death is not definite either. Twain's West lets a man play many parts and experience many things; death cannot be a serious threat to such a "many-lived" man, any more than it can be to Twain's favorite animal, the "nine-lived" cat. Passing through South Pass City, a ghostly little Wyoming town in the middle of nowhere, Twain says, "The hotel-keeper, the postmaster, the blacksmith, the mayor, the constable, the city marshal and the principal citizen and property holder, all came out and greeted us cheerily, and we gave him good-day." Twain adds, "Bemis said he was a 'perfect Allen's revolver of dignities.' And he said that if he were to die as postmaster, or as blacksmith, or as postmaster and blacksmith both, the people might stand it; but if he were to die all over, it would be a frightful loss to the community" (12). Fortunately, in Twain's fictitious West, the worthy actor on the stage of South Pass City is unlikely to "die all over," any more than Orion is to be actually hanged or scalped. There is a dreamlike immunity granted to the adventures and characters in *Roughing It,* especially to many-sided Mark Twain, who presides over everything.

The opening chapters suggest the possibility of almost infinite self-development. Twain says that before departing St. Louis he "dreamed all night about Indians, deserts, and silver bars" (1). On the trip westward the stagecoach is converted into a bed, with passengers reclining upon mail bags; the coach itself is compared to a cradle: "Our cradle only rocked in a gentle, lulling way, that was gradually soothing us to sleep, and dulling our consciousness" (3). True, Twain is in for a rude awakening in the West; in the passage just quoted, his reverie is interrupted by a broken thoroughbrace. Nevertheless, a peculiar, dreamlike quality lingers throughout much of Twain's narrative, allowing for his safe expansion in the West. At times, Twain implies he will eventually awaken to a richer, fuller life; he compares sleeping in the coach to being in a cocoon (4). His narrative presents a world of metamorphoses; despite frequent harshness and disillusionment, his changes and adventures are presented with a magical assurance. Mark Twain is dreaming an amusing dream of the West.

The danger is that this dreaminess, this suggestion of infinite possibility, will cause Twain to dissipate into nothingness at last. It is another threat to his identity, adding to the threats posed by the West's polarities, illusions, and vast expanses. How many roles or selves is he to assume? How many ways is he to present himself? If not being confined to a particular self is a safeguard against limitation and death, is it not also a form of death, an inner emptiness? What government officer is Orion? Who is that man in South Pass

City? Who is Mark Twain? It is in the context of such questions that Twain strives to balance freedom and control, to allow for possibility without degenerating into either fixity or nothingness.

The cultural openness of the West presents innumerable linguistic possibilities. The West has not yet been plowed into conventional fields of grammar and meaning; consequently, there is a wilderness of talk, with peculiar growths of vernacular and dialect springing up everywhere. A woman whom Twain meets in the stagecoach is reticent at first, but blossoms dramatically when addressed:

> "Danged if I didn't begin to think you fellers was deef and dumb. I did, b'gosh. Here I've sot, and sot, and sot, a bust'n muskeeters and wonderin' what was ailin' ye. Fust I thot you was deef and dumb, then I thot you was sick or crazy, or suthin', and then by and by I begin to reckon you was a passel of sickly fools that couldn't think of nothing to say. Where'd ye come from?"
>
> The Sphynx was a Sphynx no more! The fountains of her great deep were broken up, and she rained the nine parts of speech forty days and forty nights, metaphorically speaking, and buried us under a desolating deluge of trivial gossip that left not a crag or pinnacle of rejoinder projecting above the tossing waste of dislocated grammar and decomposed pronunciation! (2)

Twain seems overwhelmed as the woman continues to talk hour after hour (she reckons herself a "sociable heifer" when conversing with equals). Later, at a stagecoach station, he is further exposed to the "vigorous new vernacular" of the West: the stage hands drink "slumgullion" and gruffly refer to one another as sons of skunks— or worse (4). Language and manners seem alien indeed in the West.

Although Twain presents himself as the suffering victim of linguistic lunacies, he also revels in such language. The "sociable heifer" is a sphinx until Twain invites her to talk; the West is silent, a vast and meaningless expanse outside the realm of language and ideas, until invited to speak, and then what is heard is the listener's own imagination. It is Twain who renders the woman's speech for us. Perhaps there never was such a woman; if there was, we don't know what her speech was really like. What matters—and what we enjoy—is Twain triumphing in his imaginative use of western vernacular. Just as he appropriates the image of the coyote, so he appropriates the vernacular of the West. Furthermore, while pretending to be confused by that vernacular, he makes it his own. Multiple dialects help make multiple selves possible; in the theatrical expansion of his persona, Twain is absorbing the words of the West and engaging in linguistic experimentation that goes far beyond his earlier western writings.

It is well known that Twain's languages show the influence of literary comedians such as Artemus Ward, Petroleum V. Nasby, and Josh Billings, who used puns, jokes, ironies, malapropisms, neologisms, cacography, quaint figures of speech, and other word games to create a linguistic free-for-all, a verbal vertigo.[10] *Roughing It* certainly shows the effect of such word games. Even more important to Twain's narrative are various western dialects, with their curious spellings and pronunciations, homely metaphors, grammatical irregularities, and disassociation from standard eastern concepts of language and logic. Taken together, freewheeling western dialects and linguistic games let Twain present language as plasticity. For Twain, language is play, at least partially free of convention, logic, and grammar, with different dialects affording various perspectives on the world. The West he creates is one of linguistic cavorting—of words, not of objects. It is a West that serves well his linguistically constructed persona.

Indeed, in *Roughing It* Twain implies that the West, his identity, and his adventures are all the result of linguistic shaping or even fabrication. Philip Burns notes that Twain's experiences are primarily linguistic: "a no-holds-barred world of linguistic possibility." Burns adds, "The western vernacular becomes a mode of experience," and "language *manufactures* reality, and this new reality then dominates human behavior."[11]

Through such shaping, Twain not only manufactures humor but also overcomes many frustrations and polarities. Nowhere is this more evident than in his anecdote about Buck Fanshaw's funeral (47). This anecdote humorously contrasts the speech of Scotty Briggs, a friend of the dead Fanshaw who is trying to arrange for his funeral, to the speech of a young minister, newly arrived from the East, who is trying to understand what Scotty wants. Scotty speaks the slang of Nevada, "the richest and the most infinitely varied and copious that had ever existed anywhere in the world, perhaps, except in the mines of California in the 'early days.'" The minister speaks the abstract, refined language of conventional Christianity. Their opening exchange typifies their entire conversation:

> "Are you the duck that runs the gospel-mill next door?"
>
> "Am I the—pardon me, I believe I do not understand?"
>
> With another sigh and a half-sob, Scotty rejoined: "Why, you see we are in a bit of trouble, and the boys thought maybe you would give us a lift, if we'd tackle you—that is, if I've got the rights of it and you are the head clerk of the doxology-works next door."
>
> "I am the shepherd in charge of the flock whose fold is next door."
>
> "The which?"
>
> "The spiritual adviser of the little company of believers whose sanctuary adjoins these premises."
>
> Scotty scratched his head, reflected a moment, and then said: "You ruther hold over me, pard. I reckon I can't call that hand. Ante and pass the buck."
>
> "How? I beg pardon. What did I understand you to say?"
>
> "Well, you've ruther got the bulge on me. Or maybe we've both got the bulge, somehow. You don't smoke me and I don't smoke you. You see, one of the boys has passed in his checks and we want to give him a good send-off, and so the thing I'm on now is to roust out somebody to jerk a little chin-music for us and waltz him through handsome."
>
> "My friend, I seem to grow more and more bewildered. Your observations are wholly incomprehensible to me. Cannot you simplify them in some way? At first I thought perhaps I understood you, but I grope now. Would it not expedite matters if you restricted yourself to categorical statements of fact unencumbered with obstructing accumulations of metaphor and allegory?"
>
> Another pause, and more reflection. Then, said Scotty: "I'll have to pass, I judge."
>
> "How?"
>
> "You've raised me out, pard."

Throughout the conversation Scotty uses figurative language based on the pastimes and occupations of himself and similar Virginia City "roughs": poker, euchre, bowling, fistfights, and mining. Many readers prefer Scotty's colorful speech to the conventional language of the minister. Indeed, Bridgman notes that Twain prefers western slang to eastern speech.

But this is a tale of two languages; Twain is fascinated by the minister's speech as well. Philip D. Beidler notes that, in Hannibal, Samuel Clemens was exposed both to "an earthy rhetoric of vernacular self-assertion" and to "another rhetoric, mainly religious, of abstract self-transcendence." Beidler believes that in the anecdote of Scotty and the minister, Twain reaches an "outright impasse" in trying to reconcile vernacular truth-telling with abstract wisdom.[12] Actually, Twain implies that both linguistic worlds are founded upon fantasy and that "truth" lies not in something clearly perceived and objectively rendered but in imaginative expressions. Far from reaching an impasse, Twain indicates that both languages are cut from figurative cloth.

When the minister enjoins Scotty to limit himself to "categorical statements of fact unencumbered with obstructing accumulations of metaphor and allegory," he is not only "raising poor Scotty out" but also ignoring what his own language does. Scotty's language is full of metaphor, allegory, and allusion; so is the minister's. For instance, the minister describes himself as "the shepherd in charge of the flock whose fold is next door." His conversation with Scotty is not so much a clash of correct versus slang as it is an engagement between different symbolic systems, which is especially apparent when Scotty and the minister speak of death:

> "Now we're all right, pard. Let's start fresh. Don't you mind my snuffling a little—becuz we're in a power of trouble. You see, one of the boys has gone up the flume—"
> "Gone where?"
> "Up the flume—throwed up the sponge, you understand."
> "Thrown up the sponge?"
> "Yes—kicked the bucket—"
> "Ah—has departed to that mysterious country from whose bourne no traveler returns."
> "Return! I reckon not. Why pard, he's *dead!*"

Scotty first depicts death through a mining metaphor ("has gone up the flume"), then moves to a more general metaphor ("throwed up the sponge"), and finally hits upon a homely metaphor so well known that even the minister recognizes it ("kicked the bucket"). The minister, despite his professed dislike of metaphor, responds with a metaphor from *Hamlet:* death is that unknown country "from whose bourne no traveler returns." Each man frames death in terms of what he knows, be it mining or Shakespeare, poker or the Bible. "Reality" to each is largely determined by the language he uses. In *The Innocents Abroad,* Twain sees through both the Old World and the New World, recognizing the illusions and assumptions of both; in *Roughing It* he recognizes that neither the East (the minister) nor the West (Scotty) speaks objective truth, but only the truth as language and imagination create it. Whereas Twain's response in *The Innocents Abroad* is often one of disillusionment, in *Roughing It* he delights in the ways in which the West and the East make their own worlds, even if the price of creativity and linguistic play is sometimes misunderstanding.

Moreover, the fact that both linguistic worlds are founded on fantasy and metaphor ironically allows for hope of understanding and reconciliation. It is not as though objective truth lies one way and error the other. Indeed, Scotty and the minister part with a "fraternal hand-shake" and the funeral arrangements complete. Scotty later becomes a teacher in the minister's Sunday school:

> If his Sunday school class progressed faster than the other classes, was it matter for wonder? I think not. He talked to his pioneer small-fry in a language they understood! It was my large privilege, a month before he died, to hear him tell the beautiful story of Joseph and his brethren to his class "without looking at the book." I leave it to the reader to fancy what it was like, as it fell, riddled with slang, from the lips of that grave, earnest teacher, and was listened to by his little learners with a consuming interest that showed that they were as unconscious as he was that any violence was being done to the sacred proprieties!

No violence is being done to the "sacred proprieties." Joseph was an outsider, too, with conceptual metaphors different from those of the ancient Egyptians; yet he and they eventually got along well together, as did Scotty and the minister. The important truths, it seems, are emotional ones, created from within and not the property of any given language, history, or religion; such truths may be expressed in many different ways with many different metaphors. Love, compassion, and reverence for the dead may be expressed as aptly through the metaphors of poker and mining as through those of the Bible and Shakespeare: all metaphors have their common ground in the imagination. The brawny Scotty and the "fragile, gentle, spirituel [*sic*] new fledgling," the earthy and the ethereal: both have the elements of symbol and fantasy in common. Relatively free of tradition and grammar, the West is more openly fanciful, more overtly given to playful exaggeration; but the East, the long past, is also the product of imagination. The West is an open fantasyland; the East is a covert fantasyland. Like Scotty and the minister, West and East are not really polarities after all—they meet in the imagination.

Twain implies that, westerner or easterner, a human being is often a fantasizing creature, his imagination permeating his language and sense of the world. Because a person's sense of himself is couched in language, his identity is also the product of imagination. For Twain, imagination offers a way of transcending disappointments and divisions based on incongruous, irreconcilable "facts"; different lands, languages, and customs offer Twain different ways to express himself. Despite linguistic discords, the Scotty Briggs anecdote is a joyous harmony. We are not to *choose* between these two languages, or any other languages; instead, we are to become imaginatively inclusive, coming to understand differing systems of metaphor, as Scotty and the minister come to understand each other.[13]

Released from the obsession with making "correct" decisions, Twain is free to enjoy the linguistic openness of the West. A few chapters after the Scotty Briggs anecdote, Twain suggests the creative sportiveness of fantasy, the West, and life in general. In the anecdote of Jim Blaine and his grandfather's old ram, Twain presents a storyteller drunk with whiskey and imagination (53). Sitting atop an empty powder keg, Blaine narrates a tale that we expect every moment will explode into meaning, or at least come to the supposed subject (the old ram). Instead, Blaine's narration continually implodes into his own freewheeling subconscious mind. Purporting to be about the objective world and based on remembrance of facts, Blaine's tale instead is introspection made dramatic monologue, fantasy masking as memory, with characters and events manufactured at will. With his round and serious face, Blaine hoaxes those who are expecting a conventional story and meaning. Indeed, Blaine gives us a tale that, in its wild associations and seeming randomness, is a paradigm for the impulsive fecundity of life. The ending of the narrative is indicative of the whole:

> Parson Hagar belonged to the Western Reserve Hagars; prime family; his mother was a Watson; one of his sisters married a Wheeler; they settled in Morgan County, and he got nipped by the machinery in a carpet factory and went through in less than a quarter of a minute; his widder bought the piece of carpet that had his remains wove in, and people come a hundred mile to 'tend the funeral. There was fourteen yards in the piece. She wouldn't let them roll him up, but planted him just so—full length. The church was middling small where they preached the funeral, and they had to let one end of the coffin stick out of the window. They didn't bury him—they planted one end, and let him stand up, same as a monument. And they nailed a sign·on it and put—put on—put on it—sacred to—the m-e-m-o-r-y—of fourteen y-a-r-d-s—of three-ply—car - - - pet—containing all that was—m-o-r-t-a-l—of—of—W-i-l-l-i-a-m—W-h-e— (53)

There's no closure to Jim Blaine's narrative: he begins to drowse over the words "put on" (which this anecdote surely is) and finally falls asleep over the name *Wheeler*. One suspects that if he did not fall asleep, Blaine could wheel out his narrative endlessly, spinning fantastic yarns and associations. Like Wheeler's coffin, Blaine is not confined by traditional structures—both "stick out of the window," so to speak. In fact, *Roughing It* as a whole sticks out of the window, escaping customary frameworks of logic, belief, and narrative pattern.

Twain captures in Blaine's narrative the seeming randomness of both imagination and life—often a frightening prospect, with the threat of anarchy both within and without. The West, largely unregulated by conventional rules, magnifies the indeterminacy of life: Wheeler is nipped through the carpet machine; Twain is sucked through a series of fantastic adventures in *Roughing It*. Just as it would be hard to find a "moral" (or even the ram!) in Blaine's narrative, so we may fear that both life and Twain's book lack meaning and direction.

Yet consider the words of Jim Blaine, midway through his meandering narrative: "But mind you, there ain't anything ever reely lost; everything that people can't understand and don't see the reason of does good if you only hold on and give it a fair shake; Prov'-

dence don't fire no blank ca'tridges, boys. . . . There ain't no such a thing as an accident." His words are ironic, given his tale; Wheeler, if he could be unwoven from his carpet, might question whether "there ain't no such a thing as an accident." Indeed, everything seems accidental, irrational, or incongruous in this freewheeling narrative of fantasies: nothing "fits right," whether it is Miss Wagner's borrowed glass eye or the fact that a Baptist deacon, old Thankful Yates, is a cattle rustler. Despite all the chaos of Blaine's tale, however, there is a design, an achievement of significance. Although Blaine never arrives at his stated purpose, the story of the old ram, he gives us an entertaining anecdote nonetheless. Within chaos may be order; serendipity may be structure. Imagination can take randomness and incongruities and convert them into the play of humor.

In *The Innocents Abroad,* Twain experiments in various ways with transforming disorder into humor, as in the "Ascent of Vesuvius" passages, but only in *Roughing It* does he blend chaos and control. He implies that life itself—with its mishaps, incongruities, peculiar associations, and commingling of order and anarchy—parallels the workings of the subconscious mind, especially in its dream states. The fertilely chaotic life of the West parallels Twain's fantasy-making. By incorporating more and more of life's anarchic abundance, Twain is led not into hopeless disorder but into a humorous celebration of creativity. Twain's humor becomes a form of order based on inventive association.

This understanding of how fantasy permeates life leads Twain to extend his humorous treatment, to play with ways by which the plasticity of fiction may suggest the plasticity of the past. He experiments with how memory works, with how a sense of the past is evoked. A distinguishing feature of the West is its relative lack of a recorded past—a feature that lets western writers such as Twain invent and reinvent that past. In many ways the indeterminacy of the West's past reflects the indeterminacy of history. History can also be a matter of fantasy. In *The Innocents Abroad,* Twain suggests that the past may be shaped, but not until *Roughing It* does he experiment fully with this idea. Aboard the Sandwich Islands–bound steamer, *Ajax,* he introduces us to a bluff, eccentric old whaling captain who manufactures history. The Admiral, as he is known, invents historical "facts" to support the Confederacy, which he backs because he sees it as an underdog. Imagination being more flexible and forceful than memory, the Admiral vanquishes all opponents—until a meek man named Williams returns fantasy for fantasy:

> Now I grant you that what you have stated is correct in every detail—to-wit: that on the 16th of October, 1860, two Massachusetts clergymen, named Waite and Granger, went in disguise to the house of John Moody, in Rockport, at dead of night, and dragged forth two Southern women and their two little children, and after tarring and feathering them conveyed them to Boston and burned them alive in the State House square; and I also grant your proposition that this deed is what led to the secession of South Carolina on the 20th of December following. . . . But Admiral, why overlook the Willis and Morgan case in South Carolina? You are too well informed a man not to know all about that circumstance. . . . On the 12th of August, 1860, *two months* before the Waite and Granger affair, two South Carolina clergymen, named John H. Morgan and Winthrop L. Willis, one a Methodist and the other an Old School Baptist, disguised themselves, and went at midnight to the house of a planter named Thompson—Archibald F. Thompson, Vice President under Thomas Jefferson,—and took thence, at midnight, his widowed aunt, (a Northern woman,) and her adopted child, an orphan named Mortimer Highie, afflicted with epilepsy and suffering at the time from white swelling on one of his legs, and compelled to walk on crutches in consequence; and the two ministers, in spite of the pleadings of the victims, dragged them to the bush, tarred and feathered them, and afterward burned them at the stake in the city of Charleston. . . . And you remember also, that this thing was the *cause* of the Massachusetts outrage. Who, indeed, were the two Massachusetts ministers? and who were the two Southern women they burned? I do not need to remind *you*, Admiral, with your intimate knowledge of history, that Waite was the nephew of the woman burned in Charleston; that Granger was her cousin in the second degree, and that the women they burned in Boston were the wife of John H. Morgan, and the still loved but divorced wife of Winthrop L. Willis. (62)

Williams praises the Admiral's sense of fairness and asks him to acknowledge the justice of the argument; the Admiral, vanquished, retreats behind the pilothouse, where he is reported to have "'ripped and cursed all to himself' till he loosened the smoke-stack guys and becalmed the mainsail."

Here Twain combines fantasy with plausibility, absurdity with concrete detail. The fantasizing mind *makes* history, parodying our customary interpretations (and inventions) of the past. Indeed, history itself, full of mishaps, ironies, and irrationalities, is shown to have all the seeming of a dream—or nightmare. Williams's anecdote is no more incongruous and bloody than many of the events of the Civil War. Fantasy, chaos, and violence seem everywhere; the "facts" of history dissolve.

What is particularly fascinating about Williams's anecdote is how the Admiral is entangled in its lies and forced to grant authority to them. Williams entraps the Admiral by agreeing to enter the fictional world the Admiral has created and then ensnares the Admiral within that world. The Admiral, by sticking to the fictional conditions he has created (and he has no choice unless he admits that his "facts" are inventions), is thus forced to play by the rules of his own game, even when those rules are used against him by a superior player. The Admiral becomes so ensnared that he cannot openly challenge Williams's invented history. Perhaps he is unable to challenge it even in his own mind. Having rested his sense of "reality" upon his own fictional history of the war's causes, the Admiral may be unable to resist Williams's fictions. The line between "fiction" and "reality" is blurred by the game-playing tendencies of the Admiral's own mind.

Williams invents history that is even more "real," more concrete and detailed, than that invented by the Admiral. In fact, so precise is it as to names, dates, family connections, motives, and events that in some ways it is realer than reality itself, analogous to the modern art movement known as superrealism, in which painted objects have such a stark objectivity that they seem more real than actual objects.[14] Accordingly, Williams's narrative further confuses the Admiral. So confident is Williams of his skill that he even gratuitously tosses in a blatant untruth, namely, that one Archibald F. Thompson was vice president under Thomas Jefferson; the Admiral is helpless to contest it. Other details may not be as open to summary rejection but are nonetheless, in their outrageousness or humorous absurdity, clearly fictional. The Admiral is unable to challenge even openly nonsensical statements.

The Admiral isn't the only one entrapped by invented history. Through Williams, Twain leads the reader to consider that he himself is entrapped by the collective fictionalization of history. By the time of *Roughing It*, apologist histories of the Civil War were already appearing. Such blatant examples of fictionalization are not confined to that era: there have been various fictionalized histories of more recent wars, from World War I to Vietnam. History texts often suggest the difficulty, if not impossibility, of disentangling "fact" from "interpretation." This problem pertains even to the most fundamental issues of our history and identity as a people—for instance, is it a "fact" or an "interpretation" that Americans are a chosen people and spread across the West according to a Manifest Destiny? The Admiral and Williams both express, in exaggerated form, the ways people "sense" history and try to support that sense with conscious or unconscious fictionalizations.

The West, with its relatively unrecorded history, with its tall tales about how it was "won," with its history constantly invented anew, is once again an example writ large. The Admiral and Williams are versions of the western teller of tall tales, versions of Jim Blaine, except that their tales concern national history, not Miss Wagner's borrowed glass eye. Twain's tale of the Admiral and Williams introduces the Sandwich Islands section of the book; the anecdote about Markiss, the supreme liar, closes it. The two anecdotes thus serve to "frame" the Sandwich Islands section within the book (neither is found in the Sandwich Islands letters). Although the Sandwich Islands section was added mainly to fill out *Roughing It* to subscription book length and differs in many ways from the rest of the book, the two framing anecdotes relate even this section to the work's central preoccupations: how imagination and humor can illustrate the ways by which the mind manufactures its sense of reality. Twain enmeshes the reader in *Roughing It* just as Williams enmeshes the Admiral, urging him to grant certain assumptions and then holding him to those assumptions. Once the reader grants Twain the power to present the West to him, then Twain is free to present his own West, manufactured history and all, controlled solely by himself. The creator of Blaine, the Admiral, and Williams, Twain becomes the shaper of "reality" in his book, which allows almost infinite comic possibilities.

With such potentiality, however, also comes the possibility of chaos, even oblivion. The West is such an obvious void for Mark

Twain that it leads him to consider the void hidden in all places and all life, including the void in Samuel Clemens. Fender remarks, "In the West Clemens first looked over the brink, first confronted the possibility that he was, and would be, nothing; that not only he, but perhaps human society itself, was finally nothing."[15] This point has perhaps deeper ramifications than Fender realizes, for *Roughing It* indicates not so much Samuel Clemens's concern with social definitions of "success" as Mark Twain's concern with what it means to "be," how "reality" is made by the mind, what an "I" is, and how identity—specifically, his identity as a literary personality—may be created. It may not be possible for Samuel Clemens to alter the facts of his life and psychological makeup, but Mark Twain is free to make his narrative and himself—free to shape the image that he presents to readers in and through his work. Shaping language, narrative, and history, Twain responds to the void of the West and of life in general by filling it with his imaginative humor, finding and creating meaning through laughter.

Fashioning his own meanings and contexts, Twain presents himself as Gulliver, discovering new realms in order to illuminate old problems. He looms large over the world he controls:

> I do not remember where we first came across "sage-brush," but as I have been speaking of it I may as well describe it. This is easily done, for if the reader can imagine a gnarled and venerable live oak tree reduced to a little shrub two feet high, with its rough bark, its foliage, its twisted boughs, all complete, he can picture the "sage-brush" exactly. Often, on lazy afternoons in the mountains, I have lain on the ground with my face under a sage-brush, and entertained myself with fancying that the gnats among its foliage were lilliputian birds, and that the ants marching and countermarching about its base were lilliputian flocks and herds, and myself some vast loafer from Brobdingnag waiting to catch a little citizen and eat him. (3)

Despite his frequent pose of naïveté in the early chapters, Twain exerts comic mastery over his adventures. Even his account of the disorienting trip west is under control—unlike his narrative of the *Quaker City* voyage, when Twain sometimes expresses confusion and irritation. Granted, the stagecoach on the oceanlike prairie is subject to rocking and discomfort, as was the *Quaker City,* but Twain's presentation renders this disturbance humorous:

> Every time we avalanched from one end of the stage to the other, the Unabridged Dictionary would come too; and every time it came it damaged somebody. One trip it "barked" the Secretary's elbow; the next trip it hurt me in the stomach, and the third it tilted Bemis's nose up till he could look down his nostrils—he said. The pistols and coin soon settled to the bottom, but the pipes, pipe-stems, tobacco and canteens clattered and floundered after the Dictionary every time it made an assault on us, and aided and abetted the book by spilling tobacco in our eyes, and water down our backs. Still, all things considered, it was a very comfortable night. (4)

The tone is noticeably lighter in *Roughing It* than in *The Innocents Abroad.* Bemis's remark that he can now look down his own nostrils easily dispels the idea that he was distressed at having a six-pound unabridged dictionary up his nose; Twain is able to conclude that, all in all, "it was a very comfortable night." The pattern is set for Twain's handling of many discomforts, disjunctions, and disillusionments in his narrative; despite its title and subject matter, *Roughing It* is a "very comfortable" book for both narrator and reader because the West's harshness and dichotomies are controlled by Twain's comic impulse.

Indeed, Twain makes the West safe for himself and the reader. Bridgman notes that *"Roughing It* is a book of high energy, of mostly cartoon violence."[16] Like cartoon violence, the violence of *Roughing It,* no matter how explosive it may be, is not threatening. Because Twain's West is of the mind and "the mind is its own place," Twain controls the West's threats. His mastery is shown in the tale of Tom Quartz, the cat. This anecdote's narrator, Dick Baker, is in some ways a projection not only of Twain but also of what he fears most about the West. Ghostly, haunting the now-deserted mining camps of once-prosperous Calaveras County, Baker shows what the illusions and disappointments of the West may reduce one to. Yet the anecdote that Baker relates about Tom Quartz is ultimately one of triumph, not defeat.

Baker begins by describing how Tom Quartz, "the remarkablest cat *I* ever see," knew more about pocket mining than any man alive.

According to Baker, the trouble began when the miners gave up pocket mining (an unusual type of placer mining) and began to sink shafts in search of quartz veins. Tom Quartz, who loved the old ways of mining, looked suspiciously upon the "new fangled" quartz mining that was producing debts but not much else. After a while, however, the cat began coming into the shaft to investigate. One day the miners lit a dynamite fuse, unaware that Tom was in the shaft. Tom was blown sky-high, and when he came down, he was none too happy:

> Well, I reckon he was p'raps the orneriest lookin' beast you ever see. One ear was sot back on his neck, 'n' his tail was stove up, 'n' his eye-winkers was swinged off, 'n' he was all blacked up with powder an' smoke, an' all sloppy with mud 'n' slush f'm one end to the other. . . . He took a sort of a disgusted look at hisself, 'n' then he looked at us—an' it was just exactly the same as if he had said—"Gents, maybe *you* think it's smart to take advantage of a cat that ain't had no experience of quartz minin', but *I* think *different*"—an' then he turned on his heel 'n' marched off home without ever saying another word.
>
> That was jest his style. An' maybe you won't believe it, but after that you never see a cat so prejudiced agin quartz mining as what he was. (61)

When Twain asks if Baker was ever able to cure the cat of his "remarkable" prejudice against quartz mining, Baker replies, "*Cure him!* No! When Tom Quartz was sot once, he was *always* sot—and you might a blowed him up as much as three million times 'n' you'd never a broken him of his cussed prejudice agin quartz mining." Twain notes "the affection and the pride that lit up Baker's face when he delivered this tribute to the firmness of his humble friend of other days."

Baker has given his own characteristics to the cat. Tom Quartz's distrust of the "new fangled" quartz mining, his love of old habits, his getting "the blues" and worrying about bills piling up, and his disgust with the results of quartz mining all reflect Baker's own feelings. When Baker pays tribute to the cat's eternal dislike of quartz mining and his potential ability to survive as many as 3 million explosions, he may be making a statement about himself, ghostly exile though he is, and about his own ability to adapt to the changeful experience of the West. And through this anecdote, we see Mark Twain. Like Tom Quartz, Twain often wonders "what in the Dickens it was all about"; also like Tom Quartz, Twain survives the most incredible adventures, though sometimes a bit worse for wear.

Twain controls not only the explosions of the West but also its frequent monotony and heartbreak. Where the arid West lacks creativity, Twain waters it with his own. Allegedly forced to listen many times to an anecdote about stagecoach driver Hank Monk, who once took Horace Greeley to his destination on time but roughly, Twain makes repetition itself into a joke and freely exaggerates the story's ubiquity and the western desire to tell it. At Twain's request, one poor invalid refrains from telling the tale, but the strain is too much and he dies. Twain concludes:

> I am aware, now, that I ought not to have asked of the sturdiest citizen of all that region, what I asked of that mere shadow of a man; for, after seven years' residence on the Pacific coast, I know that no passenger or driver on the Overland ever corked that anecdote in, when a stranger was by, and survived. . . . I have had the same driver tell it to me two or three times in the same afternoon. It has come to me in all the multitude of tongues that Babel bequeathed to earth, and flavored with whisky, brandy, beer, cologne, sozodont, tobacco, garlic, onions, grasshoppers—everything that has a fragrance to it through all the long list of things that are gorged or guzzled by the sons of men. . . . Bayard Taylor has written about this hoary anecdote, Richardson has published it; so have Jones, Smith, Johnson, Ross Browne, and every other correspondence-inditing being that ever set his foot upon the great overland road anywhere between Julesburg and San Francisco; and I have heard that it is in the Talmud. I have seen it in print in nine different foreign languages; I have been told that it is employed in the inquisition in Rome; and I now learn with regret that it is going to be set to music. I do not think that such things are right. (20)

In this chapter, Twain inflicts the Monk-Greeley anecdote upon the reader four times, with nary a variation. Yet, because of Twain's framing and control of the anecdote, the whole episode is hilarious. Repetition becomes creation. In a footnote concluding the chapter, Twain laments that the Monk-Greeley anecdote has no basis in fact and that the famous—or infamous—stagecoach ride never occurred.[17] He adds, "If it were a good anecdote, that seeming demerit would be its chiefest virtue, for creative power belongs to greatness; but what ought to be done to a man who would wantonly contrive so flat a one as this? If *I* were to suggest what ought to be done to him, I should be called extravagant—but what does the thirteenth chapter of Daniel say? Aha!" One is left to wonder if the frequent tellings of the anecdote ever occurred. There is no thirteenth chapter of Daniel.[18]

Twain plays off the West's hoaxes, turning them into *his* hoaxes. In earlier narratives Twain pitted illusions against one another and made use of hoaxes; not until *Roughing It,* however, does he exert such control that he converts external hoaxes into internal ones, with hardly a seam to indicate the difference. That is, he makes the West's hoaxes his own without altering the nature of the original hoax. For instance, the Mormons, whose religion and lifestyle Twain regards as fraudulent and absurd—a hoax perpetrated on themselves and others—become, through Twain's caricature of Brigham Young, Twain's own hoax. Following the Mormon belief in polygamy, Brigham Young has many wives—and so Twain renders for us the problems of a man with so many wives and children. Twain "distances" the anecdote by ascribing it to "a Gentile by the name of Johnson," as though to suggest authority for it. Johnson's tale tells of Brigham Young's trials and tribulations: if one wife receives a breast pin, all the other wives want one exactly the same; if one child receives a tin whistle, all the other children (of which there are 110) want one too, and blow their whistles at all hours. Unknown women and their children pass themselves off as his, and the expenses mount up. Brigham Young tries to save money by building a communal bed, but he declares it a failure:

> I could *not* sleep. It appeared to me that the whole seventy-two women snored at once. The roar was deafening. And then the danger of it! That was what I was looking at. They would all draw in their breath at once, and you could actually see the walls of the house suck in—and then they would all exhale their breath at once, and you could see the walls swell out, and strain, and hear the rafters crack, and the shingles grind together. (15)

Twain gives the game away with wild exaggerations at the end; but for most of Johnson's narrative, absurd though it may sometimes seem, we have to grant a certain fantastic plausibility to it. After all, Brigham Young *would* have had bizarre difficulties with so many wives and children. Twain just extrapolates a bit, so to speak, and turns what he sees as the nonsense of polygamy into his own nonsense. An exterior absurdity becomes his interior nonthreatening property, upon which he builds his humor.

Perhaps the best example of how Twain converts the West's hoaxes and absurdities into his own is his anecdote about the "blind lead." Twain presents himself as a millionaire for ten days when he and a comrade, Calvin Higbie, discover a blind lead off the rich Wide West mine in Esmeralda, stake a claim with a third partner, A. D. Allen, but then lose the claim because they fail to work it within ten days (40, 41). Samuel Clemens probably never had this experience, at least not in the form narrated here.[19] What matters is that Mark Twain may own and lose such a mining claim in his narrative; he defines his "reality" for us. Yet the narrative reality is also open to question here, for we should be suspicious of a melodramatic tale in which both Twain and Higbie, through a series of incredibly untimely diversions, arrive at the claim site just minutes too late to keep others from possessing it. That is, within the context of the narrative itself, this anecdote suggests at least some deception. When Twain declares, "It reads like a wild fancy sketch, but the evidence of many witnesses, and likewise that of the official records of Esmeralda District, is easily obtainable in proof that it is a true history" (41), he protests too much, and he thereby prompts us to wonder what "proof" or "true history" means. Moreover, when we speculate upon a story about a *blind* lead in a mine named the Wide West, we cannot help but wonder if we aren't reading an allegory of—and a hoax on—the West itself and our conceptions of it. Twain takes the central illusion of the West, the seemingly easy prospect of sudden wealth, and converts it into his own dramatic fiction.

The hoax may run deeper. The dedication of *Roughing It* reads, "To CALVIN H. HIGBIE, of California, an Honest Man, a Genial Comrade, and a Steadfast Friend, THIS BOOK IS INSCRIBED by the Author, in Memory of the Curious Time When We Two WERE MILLIONAIRES FOR TEN DAYS." Samuel Clemens, *as Mark Twain*, is quite possibly dedicating the entire book to a hoax, or at any rate to a considerable exaggeration, since the evidence suggests that Clemens and Higbie were never millionaires (that is, they never actually owned a rich mine). For those tempted to confuse Twain's narrative with Clemens's experiences, much of Twain's "memory" of the West may be a hoax, for often he is not remembering what happened to Clemens so much as he is inventing or at least exaggerating: we gain the fictions of Mark Twain, not the memories of Samuel Clemens. Yet perhaps the deepest level of the hoax is that on one plane it is not a hoax at all. As "created memory" it is truer than memory itself; it is true for both Mark Twain and Samuel Clemens because the blind lead anecdote captures the essence of the West—its exaggerated promises of wealth and fame. Twain has made an integral hoax of the West his own, has given us "invented experience," a contradiction and yet not a contradiction, for he has also given us a truth about the West. His aptitude for creating "memories" truer than actual memories will serve him well in *Tom Sawyer, Life on the Mississippi,* and *Huckleberry Finn.*

In *Roughing It,* Twain suggests the difficulty of distinguishing the boundary between mind and world; his preoccupation with fantasy leads him to consider how the mind shapes experience. Indeed, he shows that the mind tends to transform almost every impression into exaggeration or invention. The dark side of this process is fanatical delusion, in which a given notion is pushed to an overbearing extreme—the western obsession with "striking it rich," for example. The bright side is humor, fantasy, and fun. By shaping language, history, and even basic conceptions of reality, *Roughing It* illustrates the play of the mind—the restless, pioneering tendency of the mind not to stay settled with a given idea but to push at that idea, transforming and expanding it into new frontiers. That is, the mind takes an idea or experience and infuses it with personal fantasy and emotional content—sometimes more, sometimes less, sometimes consciously, sometimes unconsciously. The result may be exaggeration, even pure fantasy, but one is often puzzled to say at just what point imagination supersedes reality. Twain implies that the mind works so naturally toward invention that one may be far along in the process before he realizes, if ever, what has happened. He may then return to some base, some supposed rock of fact, only to begin the process again. In short, Twain suggests that the mind fashions its world. For Twain, this process is liberating, despite the dangers of obsession and disorientation.

The play of the mind is shown in Twain's description of a Washoe Zephyr blowing through Carson City:

> This was all we saw that day, for it was two o'clock, now, and according to custom the daily "Washoe Zephyr" set in; a roaring dust-drift about the size of the United States set up edgewise came with it, and the capital of Nevada Territory disappeared from view. Still, there were sights to be seen which were not wholly uninteresting to new comers; for the vast dust-cloud was thickly freckled with things strange to the upper air—things living and dead, that flitted hither and thither, going and coming, appearing and disappearing among the rolling billows of dust—hats, chickens and parasols sailing in the remote heavens; blankets, tin signs, sage-brush and shingles a shade lower; door-mats and buffalo robes lower still; shovels and coal scuttles on the next grade; glass doors, cats and little children on the next; disrupted lumber yards, light buggies and wheelbarrows on the next; and down only thirty or forty feet above ground was a skurrying storm of emigrating roofs and vacant lots. (21)

If we compare this passage with references to the Washoe Zephyr in Twain's earlier writings, we see many more details and a developed sense of gradation. The Washoe Zephyr might be a metaphor for the mind itself, with its different grades or layers of consciousness, distortion, and exaggeration. By the time we arrive at the lines describing lumberyards, roofs, and vacant lots blowing through the air, we are in the land of fantasy; but we can't be sure exactly when or how we got there. We don't know just when Twain glides from observation to exaggeration. Twain's description of the Washoe Zephyr does have a certain logic, with progressively heavier objects occupying progressively lower levels in the dust storm. He incorporates our sense of gravity into a passage that nonetheless is full of light fantasy and humor. He implies that our mind naturally transforms many objects and ideas into comic exaggerations or fantasies.

Twain comments about the Washoe Zephyr: "It was something to see that much. I could have seen more, if I could have kept the dust out of my eyes" (21). The point is that the mind is often throwing dust into our eyes, causing us to see flying lots where they are not. Twain follows the Washoe Zephyr passage with humorous accounts that blow dust over lines of demarcation. His estimable "French" landlady is named Bridget O'Flannigan; the aristocracy and the "common herd" living in her boardinghouse are separated only by partitions made of flour sacks; and the governor provides "recreation" for his camp followers by sending them out into the desert to do meaningless survey work. The surveyors bring tarantulas back to the boardinghouse. Twain blurs the distinction between arachnid and human: "When their feelings were hurt, or their dignity offended, they were the wickedest-looking desperadoes the animal world can furnish. If their glass prison-houses were touched ever so lightly they were up and spoiling for a fight in a minute. Starchy?—proud? Indeed, they would take up a straw and pick their teeth like a member of Congress" (21). Before we know it, we have slid from tarantulas to congressmen; the line between nonhuman and human shimmers and vanishes. Twain is not restricted by conventional distinctions; all is alike material for his humor, letting him innovate associations, analogies, and metaphors.

Looking out over the vast western landscape, Twain may have noted that lines of demarcation disappear. Where does Nevada Territory end and California begin? The West shows that the mind maps out lines on reality, only to erase or transgress them. Twain's narrative about the West becomes a narrative about the mind, showing that categories may be dissolved and remade. In Bemis's buffalo anecdote, mental frolicking is at its liveliest. The owner of the "cheerful" Allen revolver, Bemis invents a tall tale to cover his cowardice during a buffalo hunt. What "truth" we have is that Bemis, chased by a wounded buffalo bull, left his horse and climbed a tree. But in Bemis's anecdote imagination takes over, blurring distinctions between truth and lies, people and animals. Bemis projects his fear onto his horse, ascribing all sorts of ludicrous terrors to the animal: "I wish I may die if he didn't stand on his head for a quarter of a minute and shed tears." Declaring he was literally carried away by the terrified animal, Bemis says that when he was finally thrown to the ground, he climbed a nearby tree. Bemis also ascribes various human attributes to his enemy, the wounded buffalo bull: "I watched the bull, now, with anxiety—anxiety which no one can conceive of who has not been in such a situation and felt that at any moment death might come. Presently a thought came into the bull's eye. I knew it! said I—if my nerve fails now, I am lost. Sure enough, it was just as I had dreaded, he started in to climb the tree" (7). Bemis projects his cunning onto the bull's mind, just as he projects his fear onto his horse. In effect, he breaks down distinctions between subject and object, mind and world, making the world conformable to his wishes and humor. Reality is transformed into an expression of Bemis's inventive mind. When his listeners try to reimpose an external order by asking Bemis how his saddle got up into the tree with him (Bemis claims he hanged the bull with the lariat from his saddle), Bemis is quick to invent anew, saying the saddle fell into the tree after his horse bucked it. Similarly, to his listeners' charge that a bull can't climb a tree, Bemis replies that just because they haven't seen a bull do it does not mean it can't be done.

After Bemis ends his anecdote, there follows this exchange between him and his listeners:

> "Bemis, is all that true, just as you have stated it?"
> "I wish I may rot in my tracks and die the death of a dog if it isn't."
> "Well, we can't refuse to believe it, and we don't. But if there were some proofs—"
> "Proofs! Did I bring back my lariat?"
> "No."
> "Did I bring back my horse?"
> "No."
> "Did you ever see the bull again?"
> "No."
> "Well, then, what more do you want? I never saw anybody as particular as you are about a little thing like that." (7)

This conversation recalls the Adam's tomb passage in *The Innocents Abroad,* in which Twain both mocks and celebrates the way the mind may glide from logic to illogic. In *Roughing It* the process is more subtle, more reflective of the mind's intricate play. Bemis's use of "negative evidence" (You don't see my lariat; therefore, my story, which accounts for the lariat's disappearance, must be true) dissolves demarcations between logic and illogic, evidence and fabrication, reason and imagination. Bemis's anecdote and *Roughing It* as a whole indicate that we often "account" for things by fitting them into an explanatory "story," with the story then becoming our evidence or explanation for why these things are as we say they are. By transforming his fabrications into a story, by providing them with a narrative framework, Bemis implies that they become factual. Play becomes reality. The only reason most of us scoff at Bemis's story is we are sure bulls can't climb trees.

But what if bulls could climb trees? In an anecdote immediately following Bemis's story, Twain gives us the next best thing: a cat that eats coconuts. Twain tells a tale about an Englishman named Eckert in Siam, "famous for the number, ingenuity and imposing magnitude of his lies," who is constantly being solicited to tell another whopper, yet rarely will do so before strangers. Twain's friend, Bascom, explains that he has a way to draw Eckert out: "Just let him have his own way. He will soon forget himself and begin to grind out lies like a mill. Don't get impatient—just keep quiet, and let me play him" (7). Bascom's plan seems to work, for eventually Eckert, growing relaxed and talkative, tells of a cat that eats coconuts. While Eckert goes to fetch the cat, Bascom rejoices in his success: "Cat eat a cocoanut [*sic*]—oh, my! Now, that is just his way, exactly—he will tell the absurdest lie, and trust to luck to get out of it again. Cat eat a cocoanut—the innocent fool!" But the cat does indeed eat a coconut; in fact, it wants more. Bascom is mortified.

The anecdote punctures Bascom's claim that he can make Eckert "grind out lies like a mill"; the good, pure lie is like the wind, pursuing its own way and coming when and whence no man knoweth. The story also unsettles our notion that we can determine just when and how mental play occurs, that we can neatly distinguish fact from fiction. Probably most of us, like Bascom, believe that Eckert is lying and that no cat eats coconuts. We identify with Bascom's assumption that he knows the truth of the situation. And then we find out that he doesn't—and neither do we.

What is most disorienting is the way Twain links this anecdote to Bemis's buffalo story. At the end of Bemis's tale, Twain says, "I made up my mind that if this man was not a liar he only missed it by the skin of his teeth. This episode reminds me of an incident of my brief sojourn in Siam, years afterward." We realize that Twain is behind Bemis and his buffalo story; once again Twain poses as a passive victim of another's lies when in fact he is both creator and controller. Twain claims Bemis is a liar and introduces the tale of Eckert as a parallel case—yet Eckert does *not* lie but tells the truth about the cat. The only lie within the anecdote is, unwittingly, Bascom's, when he says of Eckert: "I will make him lie." Who, finally, is the liar and what is the lie?

The two anecdotes taken in conjunction leave the logical reader bewildered, much like a sheet of paper on the front of which it is written: "The statement on the other side is false" and on the back of which it is written: "The statement on the other side is true." Does the cat anecdote suggest the buffalo anecdote might be true? Or does the buffalo anecdote discredit the cat anecdote? Cats climb trees, but do buffaloes eat coconuts? Or as Alice murmurs while falling down the rabbit hole, "Do cats eat bats? Do bats eat cats?"

Behind the buffalo and the cat, behind Bemis and Bascom and Eckert, is Twain, the master liar—or rather, the narrator whose lies are truths and whose truths are lies. One familiar with Samuel Clemens's life may know that he was never in Siam. But what is important is that Mark Twain *has* been there, or says he has. A created entity, Mark Twain is nonetheless "realer" than fact—"realer" even than Samuel Clemens, for Twain's narrative dominates our consciousness; it becomes the sustaining reality of *Roughing It.* Indeed, Twain plays so easily with anecdotes that we have difficulty not only in differentiating between "reality" and "illusion" but also in asserting that there *is* a difference. We may reconcile ourselves to the idea of a cat eating a coconut (after all, it does contain coconut milk), but then we reflect that Twain may be revealing his inventiveness, creating both cat and coconut. That is, even within the context of the narrative we may not know what to think. Like the "blind lead" story, the buffalo and cat anecdotes invite us to accept the narrative as reality and yet also to question it—and to conclude that often we may not know what the grounds are for acceptance or rejection. For those accustomed to making sense out of a narrative through the coherence and plausibility of its parts, Twain is disorienting indeed. His fluid narrative consciousness erodes all bedrock; washed away are questions about what is "true" regarding cats, coconuts, and Clemens—and even Twain.

Nowhere is such erosion more evident than in "The Great Land-slide Case." Twain had earlier published two versions of this anec-dote—one in the *San Francisco Morning Call* on August 30, 1863, and the other in the *Buffalo Express* on April 2, 1870. The second version served as the basis for the story related in *Roughing It*.[20] In the context of the book, however, the anecdote becomes more than just a western hoax upon a pompous easterner. It undercuts human expectations of order, justice, and Providence, showing the mind's play at its mobile best.

The anecdote evidently has an outside basis. The subject of the hoax, General Buncombe ("Bombast"), is modeled on Benjamin Bunker, attorney general of Nevada Territory from 1861 to 1863. Known for his incompetence, Bunker probably was the victim of an elaborate hoax.[21] At any rate, Twain begins with a factual state-ment: The steep mountains in Nevada Territory, subject to snowmelt and spring rains, sometimes produce severe landslides. "The reader cannot know what a land-slide is, unless he has lived in that coun-try and seen the whole side of a mountain taken off some fine morn-ing and deposited down in the valley, leaving a vast, treeless, un-sightly scar upon the mountain's front to keep the circumstance fresh in his memory" (34). Twain transforms this scar of reality into the tissue of his hoax.

A rancher, Hyde, tells Buncombe that he has lost his ranch to another rancher, Morgan, because a landslide caused Morgan's ranch—buildings, fences, cattle, and all—to slide onto Hyde's ranch, covering his property "to a depth of about thirty-eight feet." Morgan, says Hyde, refuses to give up possession, claiming that he is still on his own ranch, with his own cabin and his own dirt. Hyde is understandably upset and laments his plight in tall-tale fashion:

> "And when I reminded him," said Hyde, weeping, "that it was on top of my ranch and that he was trespassing, he had the infernal meanness to ask me why didn't I *stay* on my ranch and hold pos-session when I see him a coming! Why didn't I *stay* on it, the blathering lunatic—by George, when I heard that racket and looked up that hill it was just like the whole world was a ripping and a tearing down that mountain side—splinters, and cord-wood, thunder and lightning, hail and snow, odds and ends of hay stacks,

and awful clouds of dust!—trees going end over end in the air, rocks as big as a house jumping 'bout a thousand feet high and busting into ten million pieces, cattle turned inside out and a coming head on with their tails hanging out between their teeth!—and in the midst of all that wrack and destruction sot that cussed Morgan on his gate-post, a wondering why I didn't *stay and hold possession!*" (34)

A firm believer in law and reason, Buncombe is stunned to find that almost everyone supports Morgan against Hyde. Buncombe represents Hyde in a referee court, presided over by former Governor Roop, and Buncombe gives the case his all: "He pounded the table, he banged the law-books, he shouted, and roared, and howled, he quoted from everything and everybody, poetry, sarcasm, statistics, history, pathos, bathos, blasphemy, and wound up with a grand war-whoop for free speech, freedom of the press, free schools, the Glorious Bird of America and the principles of eternal justice! [Applause.]" Roop admits that logic, evidence, and eloquence are on Buncombe and Hyde's side. He must, however, find for Morgan:

> If Heaven has chosen to favor the defendant Morgan in this marked and wonderful manner; and if Heaven, dissatisfied with the position of the Morgan ranch upon the mountain side, has chosen to remove it to a position more eligible and more advantageous for its owner, it ill becomes us, insects as we are, to question the legality of the act or inquire into the reasons that prompted it. No—Heaven created the ranches and it is Heaven's prerogative to rearrange them.

Buncombe is appalled. The most he can win from Roop is the concession that Hyde, if he so wishes, may dig his ranch out from under Morgan's. Twain concludes, "At the end of two months the fact that he [Buncombe] had been played upon with a joke had managed to bore itself, like another Hoosac Tunnel, through the solid adamant of his understanding."

Buncombe is duped. Probably he should have recognized the outrageousness of the situation, given Hyde's description of the landslide, the peculiarity that everyone sides with Morgan, and the lunacy of Roop's decision. But the matter is not so simple. After

Twain's introductory statement about the magnitude of western landslides, most readers might not be able to dismiss out of hand Hyde's claim that his ranch was covered by a landslide. Hyde's obvious exaggerations might then be ascribed to overstatement based on excitement, common in the West where imagination runs rampant anyway.

It is even more difficult to dismiss summarily Roop's ruling. As silly as his decision seems, Roop appeals to a line of reasoning that many of us have depended on at one time or another. For instance, when schools are closed by snow, it is usually deemed an "act of God," an explanation that does not differ materially from Roop's judgment that Hyde "has been deprived of his ranch by the visitation of God!" When it isn't God who is being appealed to, it is often some other "absolute," such as "natural law." Consciously or unconsciously, society and its statutes appeal at least sometimes to something "higher" to explain or justify events.[22] In such circumstances we may try to account for things by setting them in the framework of a story.

Implicit in this narrative is the suspicion that, in laughing at Buncombe, we had better be ready to laugh at ourselves as well. We glide into storytelling quite easily; we often tell stories to ourselves—some humorous, some tragic—perhaps without any final basis for determining what is real and what is not. As we go from dreaming one dream to dreaming the next, we should not regard Buncombe too contemptuously. Twain says that it took two months for the realization of the hoax to bore itself into Buncombe's mind. Should we believe that? Who is the final dupe? Pass the cat another slice of coconut.

Perhaps it doesn't matter whether the cat eats coconut, whether the buffalo hunt went as Bemis says, or whether the great landslide occurred. In the freewheeling world Twain presents to us, perhaps we should just enjoy and celebrate the mind's insistence on shaping and reshaping its world, particularly through comic narrative. We should celebrate Samuel Clemens's metamorphosis into Mark Twain and that Mark Twain cannot be strapped to any "lie detector." In effect, Twain dismisses the concept of reality. Wadlington notes about the buffalo anecdote, "To be in a really skeptical frame of mind about such a yarn as Bemis' is to be as much befooled as to be deceived by it." According to Wadlington, such stories do not raise the issue of truth or lies.[23]

Roughing It is thus devoted to transcending—or at least blurring—the reality principle. Even the Sandwich Islands section, admittedly added so as to extend *Roughing It* to the two-volume length needed for standard subscription sales, dissolves reality in play. Twain takes his newspaper letters about the islands and makes them part of his comic narrative. He considerably condenses the material: of the letters' 90,000 words, Twain uses about 30,000 and adds 5,000 of new material.[24] Everything from chapter 75 onward in *Roughing It* is new. Twain uses the anecdotes about the Admiral (62) and Markiss (77) to frame the Sandwich Islands section and put it in the context of the book. Moreover, Twain removes simplistic dualities from the original material: for instance, Brown is eliminated. Twain appropriates some of his remarks and develops an inclusive, fluid persona in place of the gentleman-vulgarian polarity. The result is that Twain can respond easily to changes in world and mood, go from romantic daydreams to daubing scorpion bites with nary a hitch, and play with life.

As Twain shows, this ability to play is crucial for enjoying life. One anecdote that Twain introduces to link the Sandwich Islands section with the rest of his narrative is about Horace Greeley and the turnips (70). Twain tells of finding a Michigan preacher trying to regain his mental and physical health on an island plantation. The unfortunate minister, Simon Erickson, has interceded on behalf of an anxious widow whose only son, "religious, amiable, and sincerely attached to agriculture," is obsessed with turnips. The boy's ambition is to make the turnip a climbing vine. Failure to accomplish this noble task eats away at him, making him as bloodless as the turnip; his desperate mother beseeches Erickson to ask Horace Greeley's advice. (In addition to being a well-known editor and political figure, Greeley was an enthusiastic amateur farmer.) Greeley responds in his notoriously bad handwriting. As nearly as poor Erickson can decipher it, the letter reads as follows: "Polygamy dissembles majesty; extracts redeem polarity; causes hitherto exist. Ovations pursue wisdom, or warts inherit and condemn. Boston, botany, cakes, folony [sic] undertakes, but who shall allay? We fear not." Now obsessed himself, Erickson tries different decodings of the letter; he gets a different "interpretation" each time, but none makes sense. Only when Erickson writes again and receives a plain copy of Greeley's letter transcribed by a clerk is the mystery cleared up. Alack and alas, by then Erickson has lost his sanity and the boy has died of a broken heart: "Poor lad, they laid him to rest with a turnip in each hand."

Twain here pokes some fun at his acquaintance Greeley. More important, Twain gives us another metaphor for life's incomprehensibility and the mind's restlessness. Bridgman notes, "Collectively, the several readings of Greeley's letter embody precisely the enigma that Twain himself had to deal with: a scrawled world that yielded a variety of uncertain and by and large unwelcome interpretations."[25] Furthermore, I suspect Greeley's letter may comically suggest the indecipherability of the world—not just to Erickson or Twain, but to all minds. Erickson's refusal to abide by any one interpretation and his relentless search for new interpretations indicate that the mind is never content with the muddle it sees in the world; rather, the mind is forever changing, adding, and searching. We inject imagination and emotion to find—or create— meaning.

We may not, however, arrive at a final or stable meaning—we may, in a sense, fail, just as Erickson does. If there is an absolute meaning to be sent down by a divine Greeley or God, it may come too late in the game to be of much point. Bridgman sees the turnip anecdote in a grim light, befitting its end in madness and death. Moreover, he sees in it Samuel Clemens's own frustration—Clemens supposedly wanted to find better human beings and to better himself, but, like the widow's son, he could not make a climbing vine out of a turnip.[26] The mind's inability to settle upon any bedrock of reality can be threatening; life's deceptive slopes can end in dangerous drops.

I suggest another reading of this anecdote. Both Erickson and the widow's son are religiously inclined; as such, they are apt to impose absolute meanings where there may be none. They want the world *their* way, to make climbing vines of turnips. Neither Erickson nor the boy can see the delightful absurdity in this idea or in Erickson's interpretations of Greeley's letter. One goes mad; the other dies. They have not learned to enjoy the fluidity of thought and the ambiguities of "reality"; they have not learned to laugh at themselves and the world. When Simon Erickson tells his story in "all earnestness," it is the sad insanity of a man who takes the world dogmatically. For him, all history is now explained by his correspondence with Greeley ("Queen Victoria wrote me that she felt just as I did about it"), just as perhaps he had tried as a minister to explain all life by a particular set of religious tenets.

Twain ends his tale of Erickson's trials thus: "So ended Erickson, and lapsed again into nodding, mumbling, and abstraction. The company broke up, and left him so. . . . But they did not say what drove him crazy. In the momentary confusion, I forgot to ask." On one level, Twain is simply being funny. On a deeper level, he suggests there really is no reason for Erickson to have gone crazy, for he faced no more incomprehensibility than each of us does every day. Couched therein is a warning to readers not to make Erickson's mistake, not to read Twain's letter to us, *Roughing It,* too dogmatically or earnestly, lest we too lapse into "nodding, mumbling, and abstraction." Samuel Clemens may or may not have found life bewildering and frustrating; Mark Twain finds pleasure and freedom in his narratives.

The Sandwich Islands section builds toward Twain's description of the huge, dead volcano of Haleakala on Maui—another passage not contained in his letters but written expressly for *Roughing It.* Standing atop the volcanic crater, Twain describes a scene that captures much of the mind of his narrative:

> Presently vagrant white clouds came drifting along, high over the sea and the valley; then they came in couples and groups; then in imposing squadrons; gradually joining their forces, they banked themselves solidly together, a thousand feet under us, and *totally shut out land and ocean*—not a vestige of *anything* was left in view but just a little of the rim of the crater, circling away from the pinnacle whereon we sat. . . . Thus banked, motion ceased, and silence reigned. Clear to the horizon, league on league, the snowy floor stretched without a break—not level, but in rounded folds, with shallow creases between, and with here and there stately piles of vapory architecture lifting themselves aloft out of the common plain—some near at hand, some in the middle distances, and others relieving the monotony of the remote solitudes. There was little conversation, for the impressive scene overawed speech. I

felt like the Last Man, neglected of the judgment, and left pinnacled in mid-heaven, a forgotten relic of a vanished world.

While the hush yet brooded, the messengers of the coming resurrection appeared in the east. A growing warmth suffused the
horizon, and soon the sun emerged and looked out over the cloud-
waste, flinging bars of ruddy light across it, staining its folds and
billow-caps with blushes, purpling the shaded troughs between,
and glorifying the massy vapor-palaces and cathedrals with a
wasteful splendor of all blendings and combinations of rich col-
oring.

It was the sublimest spectacle I ever witnessed, and I think the
memory of it will remain with me always. (76; emphasis Twain's)

Twain suggests that the mind perceives and fashions its world. This
ghostly, dreamlike quality appears elsewhere in *Roughing It;* this
passage presents an amorphous world open to imaginative shaping.
Imagination imposes form upon this world, so that one "sees" various shapes, such as the "stately piles of vapory architecture" that
rise at various distances. It is a world simultaneously abstract and
detailed, ethereal and substantial. The cloud world rolls with its val-
leys and "rounded folds" to the horizon, like the Great Plains that
Twain described earlier. When the sun rises above this clouded expanse, it creates beauty with its various lights, just as Twain's variegated imagination imparts beauty and humor to his narrative.

Atop the cloud-enwrapped volcano, Twain feels "like the Last
Man, neglected of the judgment, and left pinnacled in mid-heaven,
a forgotten relic of a vanished world." The Last Man theme figures
extensively in various later narratives, suggesting that he is outside
whatever order there may be to "reality." This passage also implies
each person's essential loneliness: in a poignant and awe-inspiring
sense, each mind actually is "its own place," creating its own awareness of the world based on its own whims, proclivities, and humors.
For Twain in *Roughing It,* the mind has a solitary grandeur, despite
its fears and confusions; its isolated supremacy grants it the solar
power of creation. The mind is able to fashion wondrous spectacles
out of the cloud mass that is the world in the same way that Mark
Twain is able to fashion humorous adventures out of the experiences of Samuel Clemens.

The mind's inventive power is celebrated by sundry critics who see *Roughing It* as a paean to humorous play and imagination. Granted, some may see this play as a conscious and sometimes distorted effort to avoid a harsh reality. For instance, Michelson contends that Twain is "actively looking for a world of make-believe" that he can defend against the painful truths that logic and objectivity would reveal. Michelson argues that the book tends to collapse in the Sandwich Islands section because play turns into work: Twain can no longer deny the oppressive presence of reality.[27] But even the Sandwich Islands material often shows the shaping power of the individual mind. It might be argued that Twain sometimes becomes darker, more strained; yet he always indicates that to think is to form one's world, for thought inevitably entails imagination. In fact for Twain, paradoxically, "reality" is the mind's ability to create "illusions," to play with the world. It is through his ability to manufacture humorous images, to make his world and himself anew, that Twain appears to us.

Although Twain does not use most of the Sandwich Islands letters in *Roughing It,* he does retain, in unaltered form, an anecdote bearing directly upon the question of identity. It is the story about Twain meeting a man who is amazed to find that Twain is not a whaler, missionary, or government official—the three main occupations on the islands. The man asks, "Then, who the mischief are you?" In the context of Twain's letters, it is a question that suggests Twain's fear of a loss of identity; he implies that to be "Mark Twain" is ultimately to be nobody. In the more confident context of *Roughing It* (66), however, it indicates Twain's ability to transcend roles and epistemological distinctions, to be a successful literary personality who cannot be categorized. Threat is converted into opportunity; this is a crucial movement from Twain's earlier writings to *Roughing It.*

This movement is another variation on Twain's search for a transcendent figure. In *Roughing It,* Twain presents various characters who cannot be classified, who seem to transcend fixed ideas. There is Slade, for example, a notorious outlaw who is nonetheless the best division-agent the Overland has ever had, a man who defies labels such as "right" or "wrong," "brave" or "cowardly" (9–11). There is the enigmatic bully "Arkansas," a man who can effortlessly distort the meaning of another man's remarks, who can intimidate a tavern full of roughs, yet who is backed down by the landlord's wife (31). There is Brigham Young, neither faker nor prophet but a strange amalgam that eludes both categories. Characters such as the Admiral and Williams transcend the distinction between "liar" and "truth-teller." And Mark Twain in his kaleidoscopic comic vision transcends our efforts to define him. He lampoons our attempts at analysis, our infatuation with logic and categories.

A common reading of *Roughing It* is that, despite its exuberance, the book is a testament of frustration and failure—an "autopsy of the American Dream," Hill calls it.[28] Certainly, Twain depicts the West not as a place to become rich but as the scene for a bewildering array of miners, roughs, speculators, and desperadoes—characters playing out strange charades in an eerie landscape that yields mica more often than gold. And there is Twain's "moral" stated at narrative's end: "If you are of any account, stay at home and make your way by faithful diligence; but if you are 'no account,' go away from home, and then you will *have* to work, whether you want to or not. Thus you become a blessing to your friends by ceasing to be a nuisance to them—if the people you go among suffer by the operation" (79).

Twain shows the heartbreak of the West. Ultimately, however, *Roughing It* transcends the West, transcends dead American dreams and timely morals; this book is about Twain's humor, discoveries, and evolution. It is about his ability to shape his language, his world, his identity. Twain may repeatedly present himself as a failure toward the narrative's end, but he does so more out of play than out of defeat; his newfound imaginative powers and developed persona let him be free and easy in such self-portrayals. He has gained power from the West. Despite the West's hardships, Twain asserts that Virginia City "afforded me the most vigorous enjoyment of life I had ever experienced" (55). Twain may show himself as humiliated, buffeted by chance, terrified before his first lecture in San Francisco, the victim of a harsh practical joke in a Nevada mountain pass (78, 79)—but he is simultaneously the confident narrator of this narrative. In short, he transmutes the trials of Samuel Clemens into the literary gold of Mark Twain. Twain says the "blind lead" adventure illustrates well his "slothful, valueless, heedless career" (40); yet we've seen that, to a considerable degree, the story is a hoax, even in the context of Twain's narrative. Twain is not blindly led—his humorous versatility provides a controlling providence for his adventures and his narrative.

At one point Twain celebrates the change of seasons, which he misses in monotonous California:

> *Change* is the handmaiden Nature requires to do her miracles with. The land that has four well-defined seasons, cannot lack beauty, or pall with monotony. Each season brings a world of enjoyment and interest in the watching of its unfolding, its gradual, harmonious development, its culminating graces—and just as one begins to tire of it, it passes away and a radical change comes, with new witcheries and new glories in its train. And I think that to one in sympathy with nature, each season, in its turn, seems the loveliest. (56)

Monotony is death. *Roughing It,* with its play of adventure, perspective, and comic technique, is life. Twain passes from mood to mood as easily and harmoniously as do the seasons he celebrates. He shows, as Beidler notes, that "consciousness, the meeting ground of linguistic and perceptual endeavor, is itself in a constant state of flux and evolution."[29] The vigor, the ecstasy of discovery, that can be found throughout *Roughing It* is not based upon the prospect of finding gold; it is based upon Twain's presentation of imaginative possibilities. Although not everyone may be able to convert western experience into comic adventure and become a highly successful author in the process, *Roughing It* suggests that the West, the world's last great fantasy playground, may offer rich revelations about one's own imagination and identity.

If there is a threat lingering in the book, it is not the threat of worthless mines but the threat that certain aspects of life may not fall under humor's dominion, no matter how developed or assertive Twain may be. Certain tragic incongruities may persist. Much of the Sandwich Islands section, which dominates the last part of the narrative, confronts the inexplicable fact of a tropical paradise pervaded by a cannibalistic past. Even in the exuberant main section of the narrative, Twain shows that his discoveries occur in a land that has meant failure and death for many.

Even more, there is the threat that Samuel Clemens, metamorphosed into Mark Twain through comic creation and the commingling of fact and fancy, may become isolated within his own imagination. Remember the story of Markiss, the consummate liar who tells many tall tales: he dies alone, having killed himself, and no one even believes in the fact of his death. Or consider again Twain's description of himself as the Last Man atop a volcanic crater in the Sandwich Islands: for all the power and beauty of the scene, there is still a ghostliness, a haunting loneliness. Even the resurrection of the sun cannot entirely abolish it. Does transcendence result in a final, supreme loneliness? Waiving questions about the psychological effect on Samuel Clemens, we may wonder whether Mark Twain may be sustained as a lofty, lone Olympian; we may wonder what limits there are to the literary imagination, the power of narration, and the process of self-creation.

In a way, *Roughing It* marks the end of a major phase of Twain's narratives. Of course, we can no more neatly categorize Twain's writings than we can carve him up into distinct parts. The quintessential Twain persists throughout all his narratives, even into the so-called dark phase. In *Roughing It,* Twain confronts and at least partially resolves various problems involving the kind of literary personality he is to be. In the middle phase of his career, beginning with *Tom Sawyer* and ending with *Huckleberry Finn,* Twain addresses the threats of isolation and ghostliness. Through imaginative re-creations of Samuel Clemens's childhood and the Mississippi valley of the 1840s and 1850s, Mark Twain indicates ways to render the world of fancy more concrete, stable, and assured. He suggests that permanence may underlie and anchor a fascination with change—a standard against which to measure change. He offers values that, while they may be created out of the human mind, may yet abide and make at least tolerable the persisting tragic disjunctions of the world. Most important, Twain becomes transcendent without fading into a detached, abstract narrative voice; his narrative mind becomes its own place without stagnating into its own prison. As he evolves, Mark Twain affirms again and again that humor may reshape world and self, offering freedom, fun, and significance.

Notes

1. The Quest for Persona and Humor

1. Van Wyck Brooks's *The Ordeal of Mark Twain* began a trend of speaking psychoanalytically of a Clemens-Twain dualism and considering how the man "Clemens" lived in conflict with the persona "Twain." Arguing that the potentially brilliant satirist Twain "sold out" to the financial worries and conventionalities of Clemens, Brooks set the terms of a seemingly endless debate. In *Mark Twain's America*, Bernard DeVoto suggested that the frontier persona of Twain actually liberated the creative abilities of Clemens, thereby providing a working harmony between self and public guise. In *Mr. Clemens and Mark Twain*, Justin Kaplan has argued much of Brooks's thesis anew, claiming that Clemens, increasingly preoccupied with business, social advancement, and progress, often found himself in a problematic relationship with the persona Twain. Even Louis Budd in *Our Mark Twain* shows how the public image of Mark Twain evolved and came to be an American symbol, though Budd sees Twain as "ultimately authentic," a basic expression of Samuel Clemens (29).

2. James M. Cox contends that Twain eventually became too serious and resorted to satire, losing his brilliantly playful humor (*Mark Twain: The Fate of Humor*, 179–84). Besides being an intriguing reversal of Brooks's lament that Twain descended from satire to mere humor and buffoonery, Cox's work typifies the critical impulse to find dualities in Twain's writings and to seek crucial "turning points" in Twain's career. For Cox, the crisis comes in Huck's decision to "go to hell" rather than betray Jim—such serious commitment makes pure humor impossible thereafter, according to Cox. Other critics have found various other turning points. For instance, many see *A Connecticut Yankee in King Arthur's Court* as marking the beginning of a descent into fragmentation and chaos. Henry Nash Smith holds that *Connecticut Yankee* shows Twain's loss of the vernacular voice and its values (*Mark Twain: The Development of a Writer*, 160–61; *Mark Twain's Fable of Progress*, 104, 107). In general, those scholars who praise Twain as a frontier or vernacular writer dislike much of his later writing; such scholars range from DeVoto to Blair to Lynn.

3. Wayne C. Booth, *The Rhetoric of Fiction,* 73, 86.

4. Sigmund Freud, "Humour," in *The Standard Edition of the Complete Psychological Works of Sigmund Freud,* 21:162; Norman N. Holland, *Laughing: A Psychology of Humor,* 107.

5. Søren Kierkegaard, *The Concept of Irony,* 37, 40, 48, 77, 236, 257–62. Similarly, Wayne C. Booth notes that "pursued to the end, an ironic temper can dissolve everything in an infinite chain of solvents" (*A Rhetoric of Irony,* 59, n. 14).

6. Kierkegaard, *Concept of Irony,* 262, 277.

7. David R. Sewell notes, "Babel lurks, Twain would come to realize, in every word of every language." Drawing upon the work of German philologist Wilhelm von Humboldt, Sewell contends that since no two people use a word exactly the same way (and the differences are even more marked between different languages), meaning is created, not merely transferred. "Thus the myth of Babel is turned on its head, and multilingualism becomes a liberation instead of a punishment" (*Mark Twain's Languages: Discourse, Dialogue, and Linguistic Variety,* 5, 84).

8. Henri Bergson, *Laughter: An Essay on the Meaning of the Comic,* 4, 10, 21, 39.

9. Johan Huizinga, *Homo Ludens,* 7, 9, 11, 13, 15, 17.

10. Holland notes a connection between humor and transcendence: "The comic catharsis, then, is (from these various Platonic or quasi-Platonic viewpoints) a resolution through transcendence of one, some, or many of the incongruities of this world (our attempts at knowledge, government, virtue, love, or riches)" (*Laughing,* 101).

11. Joseph Campbell remarks regarding the comic, "The objective world remains what it was, but, because of a shift of emphasis within the subject, is beheld as though transformed. Where formerly life and death contended, now enduring being is made manifest . . . comedy [is] the wild and careless, inexhaustible joy of life invincible" (*The Hero with a Thousand Faces,* 28).

12. Jeffrey Steinbrink (*Getting to Be Mark Twain,* xiii) notes that the persona "Mark Twain" had assumed its "essential shape" by 1871, when *Roughing It* was completed.

13. Some scholars emphasize the philosophical dimensions of Twain's later writings, instead of dismissing them as chaotic and futile efforts (as earlier critics like Smith and Lynn were wont to do). Such scholars often indicate certain motifs running throughout Twain's career, linking his earlier and later works together. Thus, Pascal Covici Jr. contends that Twain used Southwestern humor for philosophical purposes,

showing the limits of human reason, the difficulty of distinguishing illusion from reality, and the power of irrationality. Such concerns, particularly as they center on the use of illusion and hoax, provide a philosophical core to Twain's writings, Covici says (*Mark Twain's Humor: The Image of a World,* vii, 8, 13, 31, 159–60, 213, 241, and 243). These issues clearly tie Twain's later writings to the main part of his career. Other critics who similarly link Twain's early and late writings include: William Macnaughton in *Mark Twain's Last Years as a Writer;* Sholom J. Kahn in *Mark Twain's "Mysterious Stranger": A Study of the Manuscript Texts;* Mark Kosinski in "Mark Twain's Absurd Universe and 'The Great Dark'"; Louis Budd in "Mark Twain Talks Mostly about Humor and Humorists"; James C. Wilson in "'The Great Dark': Invisible Spheres, Formed in Fright"; Richard Hauck in *A Cheerful Nihilism: Confidence and "The Absurd" in American Humorous Fiction;* and David Karnath in "Mark Twain's Implicit Theory of the Comic."

2. A Washoe Zephyr

1. Mark Twain, *Mark Twain of the "Enterprise,"* ed. Henry Nash Smith and Frederick Anderson, 43.

2. For an excellent study of Samuel Clemens's early life, see Dixon Wecter, *Sam Clemens of Hannibal,* which covers the period from 1835 to 1853, when Clemens left Hannibal at age seventeen. For biographical studies of Clemens's later years, see DeLancey Ferguson, *Mark Twain: Man and Legend,* and Edward Wagenknecht, *Mark Twain: The Man and His Work.* Kaplan's *Mr. Clemens and Mark Twain,* though an excellent study, presents Clemens's life only after he returned to the East in December 1866.

3. In an October 26, 1861, letter published in the *Keokuk Gate City,* Twain writes: "Nevada Territory is fabulously rich in gold, silver, copper, lead, coal, iron, quicksilver, marble, granite, chalk, slate, plaster of Paris (gypsum), thieves, murderers, desperadoes, ladies, children, lawyers, christians, gamblers, Indians, Chinamen, Spaniards, sharpers, coyotes, (pronounced ki-yo-ties,) preachers, poets, and jackassrabbits" (*The Pattern for Mark Twain's "Roughing It,"* ed. Franklin R. Rogers, 23). See Paul Fatout, *Mark Twain in Virginia City,* and Ivan Benson, *Mark Twain's Western Years,* for good overviews of Clemens's experiences in the West.

4. Leo Marx, *The Machine in the Garden,* 45; Henry Nash Smith, *Virgin Land,* 175, 259–60.

5. Twain, *The Pattern,* 22–26. In his introduction (ibid., 1–21), the

editor discusses how these *Gate City* letters helped provide the pattern for *Roughing It.*

6. Mark Twain, *Early Tales and Sketches,* vol. 1 (1851–1864), ed. Edgar M. Branch and Robert H. Hirst, 369. See 365–66 for the editors' note on the publishing history of this piece.

7. For a typical example of his fascination with Nevada mining statistics, see Twain, *Early Tales and Sketches,* 1:415–17, which reprints an August 1863 "local column" by Twain for the *Virginia City Daily Territorial Enterprise* (ironically written only a year before many of the Nevada mines were to go "bust"). In another article, Twain writes optimistically about the mines: "From the increasing richness of the developments being made in the Hale & Norcross mine, however, I think you may count on a great advance in the price of that stock within the next few days" (ibid., 258). Of course, some of his "optimism" may have resulted from the fact that he was recompensed for "puffing" various mining stocks in his newspaper reports. In any event, it's ironic that however enthusiastic Mark Twain may have been about the mineral wealth of Nevada Territory, Samuel Clemens was poor throughout his stay (Twain, *Twain of the "Enterprise,"* 16).

8. Twain, *Early Tales and Sketches,* 1:164.

9. See Mark Twain, *Clemens of the "Call,"* ed. Edgar M. Branch, 40–42, 46–48, for samples of Twain's writing on San Francisco earthquakes and vagabond houses. For additional earthquake articles, see Twain, *Early Tales and Sketches,* vol. 2 (1864–1865), 289–310. See Mark Twain, *Letters from the Sandwich Islands,* ed. G. Ezra Dane (6–7, 9–11) for Twain's comments on equatorial calms and the monotony of shipboard life; see 206–13 for his description of Kilauea (later incorporated into *Roughing It*). Stephen Fender, "'The Prodigal in a Far Country Chawing of Husks': Mark Twain's Search for a Style in the West," 740.

10. William Dean Howells, *My Mark Twain: Reminiscences and Criticism,* 148.

11. In another context, Sewell remarks that Mark Twain recognized that "language is always potentially inflationary, since the mere substitution of one word for another increases the apparent value of the referent" (*Mark Twain's Languages,* 45).

12. Twain, *Clemens of the "Call,"* 227; Twain, *Early Tales and Sketches,* 1:258.

13. Editorial Introduction, Twain, *The Pattern,* 1–21.

14. Twain, *Early Tales and Sketches,* 1:225.

15. Ibid., 1:351–56. For the writing and publishing history of "Those Blasted Children," see the editorial introduction (347–50).

16. For good overviews on Southwestern humor, including its influence on Twain, see Walter Blair, *Native American Humor* and *Horse Sense in American Literature;* Kenneth S. Lynn, *Mark Twain and Southwestern Humor;* Constance Rourke, *American Humor;* and Jennette Tandy, *Crackerbox Philosophers in American Humor and Satire.*

17. DeVoto, *Mark Twain's America,* 94, 130.

18. Twain, *Early Tales and Sketches,* 1:275–76. Although the "wake-up-Jake" passage is clearly in the vein of frontier humor, it also closely resembles Cervantes's description of what Don Quixote's homemade "cure-all" (balsam) does to Sancho Panza (*Don Quixote,* pt. I, ch. 17).

19. Gladys Bellamy has observed the frequent theme of mental discomfort ("the humor of a mild insanity") in Twain's works (*Mark Twain as a Literary Artist,* 124). Similarly, Rourke has noted that "his fun was often half perplexity" (*American Humor,* 218). In his later writings Twain puts less emphasis on physical suffering (although he never loses his fascination with it) but becomes increasingly preoccupied with various (and more refined) forms of mental suffering.

20. See Twain, *Early Tales and Sketches,* 1:155–58 and 1:320–23, for an editorial discussion of the history of the two hoaxes; Fender, "The Prodigal," 749.

21. Mark Twain, *Contributions to the "Galaxy," 1868–1871,* ed. Bruce R. McElderry Jr., 48. That Mark Twain is inventing a hoax in this second article and is not the victim of a faulty memory is shown when he accurately quotes from his original article, indicating he has it before him.

22. Editorial introduction, Twain, *Early Tales and Sketches,* 1:321.

23. Twain, *Contributions to the "Galaxy,"* 49.

24. Ibid., 49–50.

25. Fender, "The Prodigal," 741.

26. Edgar M. Branch, *The Literary Apprenticeship of Mark Twain,* 83; William Kaufman, "The Comedic Stance: Sam Clemens, His Masquerade," 80.

27. Jacob Brackman, *The Put-on: Modern Fooling and Modern Mistrust,* 19, 20, 128; Covici, *Mark Twain's Humor,* 154, 159, 160, 183.

28. In "The Comedic Stance" Kaufman sees Samuel Clemens as having had violent tendencies but striving to suppress such feelings: "It is possible that Sam Clemens was one of the most violent men to ever have refrained from using his fists in anger, discounting one youthful intervention in a fight on his younger brother's behalf. His writings in fact depict a pervading abhorrence of physical violence, especially his own participation in it." Yet, as Kaufman adds, the humor of Mark

Twain is often filled with violence (78–79). A psychoanalytic critic might see a streak of sadomasochism in Clemens's personality, but such a theory might not contribute much to understanding the violence in Mark Twain's humor, which may have numerous causes and purposes.

29. Twain, *Early Tales and Sketches,* 1:324–25.

30. Cox, *The Fate of Humor,* 44.

31. Ibid., 10, 60, 152, 179–84; Branch, *Literary Apprenticeship,* 57–58; Benson, *Western Years,* vii; Bellamy, *Literary Artist,* 50.

32. Twain, *Early Tales and Sketches,* 1:317. As Walter Blair and Hamlin Hill note, Twain wasn't the first to use this technique to satirize newspaper reports of women's fashions; in some respects, he may have been imitating earlier sketches by John Phoenix (George Horatio Derby) (*America's Humor: From Poor Richard to Doonesbury,* 232).

33. Twain, *Early Tales and Sketches,* 2:369. Twain wasn't the only nineteenth-century American writer with such a peculiar linguistic humor; Poe once obeyed an order at West Point to appear on the parade grounds in white gloves by appearing in *only* white gloves. The incident, coupled with previous infractions, resulted in Poe's dismissal from the academy (which, of course, is what he wanted).

34. Franklin R. Rogers, *Mark Twain's Burlesque Patterns,* 26–27.

35. Twain, *Early Tales and Sketches,* 2:178.

36. Rourke, *American Humor,* 67–70.

37. Cox, *The Fate of Humor,* 103.

38. Twain, *Twain of the "Enterprise,"* 7, 97.

39. Twain, *Clemens of the "Call,"* 22.

40. Twain, *Early Tales and Sketches,* 2:36–37.

41. Harold H. Kolb Jr., "Mark Twain and the Myth of the West," 128.

42. Twain, *Clemens of the "Call,"* 214.

43. William M. Gibson, *The Art of Mark Twain,* 11; Jeffrey L. Duncan, "The Empirical and the Ideal in Mark Twain," 202.

44. Twain, *Early Tales and Sketches,* 1:176.

45. Mark Twain, *Mark Twain's Travels with Mr. Brown,* ed. Franklin Walker and G. Ezra Dane, 138; Twain, *Sandwich Islands,* 35; Twain, *Twain of the "Enterprise,"* 96.

46. Twain, *Early Tales and Sketches,* 2:24–25.

47. Mark Twain, *The Washoe Giant in San Francisco,* ed. Franklin Walker, 103.

48. DeVoto, *Mark Twain's America,* 166; Gibson, *Art of Mark Twain,* 18.

49. Branch, *Literary Apprenticeship,* 195.

50. The editors note that The Unreliable may be a precursor of Brown (Twain, *Early Tales and Sketches,* 1:249).

51. Blair, *Native American Humor,* 92; Lynn, *Southwestern Humor,* 148.

52. Branch, *Literary Apprenticeship,* 161.

53. Twain, *Sandwich Islands,* 22–24.

54. Ibid., 141–43.

55. Ibid., 156.

56. Branch, *Literary Apprenticeship,* 27.

57. John C. Gerber, "Mark Twain's Use of the Comic Pose," 297, 301–3. As Blair and Hill note (*America's Humor,* 323), Gerber's idea of "superior" and "inferior" poses corresponds to the ancient Greek concepts of "alazon" (one who pretends to be better than he is) and "eiron" (one who pretends to be less than he is).

58. Twain, *Travels with Mr. Brown,* 120–21.

59. Twain, *Sandwich Islands,* 30–31.

60. Twain, *Travels with Mr. Brown,* 118.

61. Twain, *Early Tales and Sketches,* 1:235–38. For the speculation that Perry may be the model for Buck Fanshaw, see editorial introduction to Twain, *Twain of the "Enterprise,"* 66.

62. Twain, *Travels with Mr. Brown,* 144–46.

63. For a brief discussion of Twain's literary uses of Wakeman, see *Mark Twain's Notebooks and Journals,* ed. Frederick Anderson, Michael B. Frank, and Kenneth M. Sanderson, 1:241–43.

64. Twain, *Travels with Mr. Brown,* 22. Twain's sincerity in this homage is shown by his contemporaneous notebook entry, where he declares, "I had rather travel with that old portly, hearty, jolly, boisterous, good-natured old sailor, Capt Ned Wakeman than with any other man I ever came across" (*Notebooks and Journals,* 1:253).

65. Twain, *Travels with Mr. Brown,* 30–33, 23–25, 37–38.

3. "Gazing Out over the Ocean of Time": *The Innocents Abroad*

1. The text of *The Innocents Abroad* that I'm using is the Library of America edition, ed. Guy Cardwell. All chapter citations in text are for this edition.

2. Leon T. Dickinson, "Mark Twain's Revisions in Writing *The Innocents Abroad*"; Dewey Ganzel, *Mark Twain Abroad: The Cruise of the "Quaker City"*; Mark Twain, *Traveling with the Innocents Abroad,* ed.

Daniel Morley McKeithan; Franklin Walker, *Irreverent Pilgrims: Melville, Browne, and Mark Twain in the Holy Land,* 162–224.

3. There is an added irony to the preface's claim to objectivity and truth: it is localized and dated "San Francisco, 1869," an apparent printer's error not caught by the author. The book was finished by Clemens in San Francisco in July 1868; he sailed from the city on July 6, never to see it again (Kaplan, *Mr. Clemens and Mark Twain,* 70–75).

4. Ganzel, *Mark Twain Abroad,* 123.

5. Notice the passenger list of the *Quaker City* added by the editors to Twain, *Notebooks and Journals,* 1:310–12. They note that "Blucher" is based on Frederick H. Greer of Boston.

6. John C. McCloskey, "Mark Twain as Critic in *The Innocents Abroad,*" 140–41.

7. Robert Regan bases his conclusion on an analysis of letters by Dr. Jackson, one of Clemens's companions ("the doctor"). Regan, in "The Reprobate Elect in *The Innocents Abroad,*" 248–49, notes that Clemens probably invented the incident just to have a chance to satirize the pilgrims through the "pilgrim bird."

8. Ganzel, *Mark Twain Abroad,* 234.

9. Alan Gribben, *Mark Twain's Library.*

10. Forrest G. Robinson, "Patterns of Consciousness in *The Innocents Abroad,*" 47.

11. In some later narratives Twain carries to microscopic extremes his horror at what close views reveal. In "The Great Dark" and "Three Thousand Years among the Microbes," for example, he presents nightmarish miniature worlds.

12. Allison Ensor, *Mark Twain and the Bible,* 24.

13. Philip D. Beidler argues that one of the main lessons Twain presents in *The Innocents Abroad* and *Roughing It* is that "experience" is "an ever-expanding network of associations." He also points out, much as I do, that a key problem for Twain is how to set his disjointed adventures and ideas into some context ("Realistic Style and the Problem of Context in *The Innocents Abroad* and *Roughing It,*" 35, 41).

14. Richard Bridgman (*Traveling in Mark Twain,* 15) also notes the emphasis on imprisonment in *The Innocents Abroad.*

15. Leslie Fiedler (afterword to *The Innocents Abroad,* by Mark Twain, 481) observes that Samuel Clemens "was, to be sure, the prisoner of a tour plan laid out by organizers for whom the world worth seeing had been defined once and for all by the genteel essayists of the generations before, and the writers of guidebooks, who were their degenerate heirs." I cannot, however, agree with Fiedler's additional re-

mark that Mark Twain "does not protest against the limits thus imposed."

16. Roger Salomon, *Twain and the Image of History,* 59–65.

17. Fiedler, afterword to *The Innocents Abroad,* 482.

18. Bridgman, *Traveling in Twain,* 28–29.

19. Bridgman notes that *The Innocents Abroad* "winds down through a series of endings," suggesting "Mark Twain's own uncertain commitment" (ibid., 25).

20. Bruce Michelson, "Mark Twain the Tourist: The Form of *The Innocents Abroad,*" 385–98; Cox, *The Fate of Humor,* 10, 12, 21, 44, 60; Warwick Wadlington, *The Confidence Game in American Literature,* 188–89. Wadlington notes: "In his guidebook, Twain restlessly uncovers the necessity for fashioning 'new dreams and better,' as his last significant hero will counsel in *The Mysterious Stranger*" (199).

Conversely, other critics have seen such play and humor as often ineffective in the book. Everett Emerson sees Twain's shifting perspectives as a weakness (*The Authentic Mark Twain,* 54). Similarly, in "Patterns of Consciousness," Robinson disputes the idea that Twain engages in pleasurable play, noting instead an unpleasant restlessness and the narrative's "gathering inclination to locate the source of its painful frustration not in experience but in consciousness itself" (51). And in *Traveling in Twain,* Bridgman sees the book as ending generally "weary, rancorous, and exhausted" (15).

21. The editors point out the fabricated notebook entries (Twain, *Notebooks and Journals,* 1:371–72).

4. Open Range: Persona and Humor in *Roughing It*

1. All references to *Roughing It* are to the 1993 edition in *The Works of Mark Twain* (vol. 2), ed. Harriet Elinor Smith, Edgar Marquess Branch, Lin Salamo, and Robert Pack Browning; the multivolume editor is Robert H. Hirst. All chapter citations in text are for this edition.

2. Lee Clark Mitchell observes that "the book's radical premise is that the West exists as a direction of thought" and that "only by 'roughing it' epistemologically can we begin to appreciate the fact that the West we discover is always and only our own creation" ("Verbally *Roughing It:* The West of Words," 69). Mitchell explores the linguistic landscape of *Roughing It,* and acknowledges that it was Cox who first emphasized how much the narrator shapes our view of the West in *Roughing It* (68, n. 2).

3. Twain, *Contributions to the "Galaxy,"* 91. This same Riley is the

model for the impoverished "Blucher" in chapter 59 of *Roughing It* (702, nn. 406.35–407.22). Riley also figures in chapter 26 of *A Tramp Abroad,* in the anecdote about "The Man Who Put Up at Gadsby's."

4. Twain, *Contributions to the "Galaxy,"* 107.

5. Nevada Territory's mining towns did indeed contribute nobly to this fund, but their contributions were considerably less than Twain states (Twain, *Roughing It,* 661, nn. 295.10–12, 295.14–20; 662, nn. 297.24–34).

6. Kolb, "Myth of the West," 135.

7. Editorial introduction, Twain, *The Pattern,* 1–21; Emerson, *Authentic Mark Twain,* 67; Henry Nash Smith, "Mark Twain as Interpreter of the West: The Structure of *Roughing It,*" 212.

8. Smith, *Virgin Land,* 89. Also see Smith, "Mark Twain as Interpreter," in which he argues that Twain becomes dissatisfied with the West (225). Similarly, in "Mark Twain's *Roughing It:* The End of the American Dream," Hamlin Hill declares that the West for Twain is "an initiation into homelessness, poverty, and emotional dislocation" (108). Finally, in "'Hateful Reality': The Failure of the Territory in *Roughing It,*" Tom Towers argues that "disillusionment . . . is the prevailing pattern of *Roughing It*" (4).

9. Ray Allen Billington, *Land of Savagery, Land of Promise,* 91.

10. David E. E. Sloane, *Mark Twain as a Literary Comedian,* 1–4. Sloane also traces much of Twain's egalitarianism and sense of ethics to the literary comedians. For a concise overview of the devices of the literary comedians, see Blair, *Native American Humor,* 118–23.

11. Philip Burns, "Fabrication and Faultline: Language as Experience in *Roughing It,*" 249–50, 252, 254.

12. Bridgman, *Traveling in Twain,* 35; Beidler, "Realistic Style," 40, 47.

13. It's interesting to draw a parallel here to a much later Twain work, "Extract from Captain Stormfield's Visit to Heaven." There, as Sewell points out in *Mark Twain's Languages,* the heaven that Mark Twain pictures is a "joyful mingling of voices" (154).

14. An example of superrealism is Duane Hansen's painting *The Businessman,* reproduced in O. B. Hardison Jr.'s *Disappearing through the Skylight,* 209.

15. Fender, "The Prodigal," 755.

16. Bridgman, *Traveling in Twain,* 31.

17. The Monk-Greeley stagecoach ride really did take place (July 30, 1859)—a sixty-mile trip from Nevada Territory to California. Greeley later denied it because political opponents used it to embarrass him (Twain, *Roughing It,* 609, nn. 131.13–132.6).

18. The editors point out in an explanatory note that the Catholic Bible does have a thirteenth and fourteenth chapter of Daniel—chapters that Protestants regard as apocryphal. As the editors observe, if Twain is referring to an apocryphal thirteenth chapter of Daniel, it may be to suggest that the Monk-Greeley story is also apocryphal (ibid., 612, nn. 136.5–6).

19. Although the Wide West mine did prove to have a "blind lead," there is no documentary evidence that Clemens and Higbie were involved in it; and even if they actually did locate a claim on a blind lead, they certainly did not lose it in the dramatic manner narrated. The blind lead soon turned out to be a continuation of the "Dimes" cross ledge, already located by someone else and eventually incorporated into the Wide West mine.

In "Fact and Fiction in the Blind Lead Episode of *Roughing It,*" Edgar M. Branch contends that Clemens, Higbie, and Allen did stake and lose a blind lead, but that it was a blind lead off the Pride of Utah mine, not the Wide West. Branch lacks documentary evidence, but he presents some ingenious arguments based on analysis of time frames and known events. Branch notes, however, that Clemens probably would not have been made a millionaire by such a claim (though he would have been considerably enriched) and that he did not lose the claim in the melodramatic fashion of Twain's narrative. Indeed, according to Branch, Clemens and Higbie did not return to Esmeralda until a week or more after Peter Johnson relocated the Pride of Utah blind lead on July 1, 1862.

Branch makes a thoughtful case for the basic truth of the blind lead anecdote, but disturbing difficulties remain. Branch argues that Clemens, Higbie, and Allen failed to work (and so save) their blind lead claim because they carelessly misinterpreted a very fundamental mining law; as Branch himself confesses, this explanation "seems unlikely." Clemens had been a miner for months; Higbie and Allen were evidently old hands. (Allen was foreman of the prestigious Wide West mine.) Moreover, while Branch has Clemens and his partners locating the blind lead on or about June 20, 1862, Clemens's June 22 letter to his brother, Orion, does not mention a blind lead. (Branch reproduces the first page of this letter and quotes from various parts of the whole letter.) Orion bankrolled Clemens's mining ventures, and Clemens customarily kept his brother well informed about his prospects. Clemens's June 22 letter does contain the intriguing statement: "There is an extension on the 'P. of U.,' and in order to be on the safe side, we have given them notice not to work on it."

Unfortunately, slapping an injunction against an extension of the Pride of Utah mine is a far cry from locating a blind lead. A blind lead is a *separate* or *cross* vein, not an extension of an existing (claimed) ledge. Elsewhere in the letter Clemens worries that his nearby Annipolitan claim will prove to be an extension or spur of the Pride of Utah mine and so be lost because the Pride of Utah was located (filed on) first. (When a claim is filed on a ledge or vein, it includes "all dips, spurs, and angles" of that particular vein.)

What apparently happened, in short, is that Clemens built his hopes on his nearby Annipolitan claim; it was, after all, very close to sundry rich diggings on Last Chance Hill, including both the Pride of Utah and the Wide West mines. But the Annipolitan claim either turned out to be worthless or, more likely, was lost because it proved to be part of the Pride of Utah vein (which was eventually consolidated into the Wide West mine). In other words, Clemens never actually owned a rich mine; he evidently had filed a claim on what was already part of the Pride of Utah claim and so never had legal title. In their notes to *Roughing It,* the editors (of whom Branch is one) basically adopt this perspective, though Branch's article is still cited as a reference (641–48, nn. 256.17–28 through 269.25–26). Their last note concludes that Twain's story is "at best an exaggeration." Also see George Williams III, *Mark Twain: His Life in Virginia City, Nevada,* 12–17, and *Mark Twain: His Adventures at Aurora and Mono Lake,* 49–54.

It seems most plausible that in the *Roughing It* "blind lead" anecdote Mark Twain presents a fictionalized and highly dramatized story that nevertheless expresses Samuel Clemens's actual expectations at one time of striking it rich in a mine (the Annipolitan). The hoax is that Mark Twain claims to have had and lost a rich mining claim, whereas evidently Samuel Clemens never actually owned such a claim in the first place.

20. Twain, *Roughing It,* 631, n. 220.2; Mark Twain, *The Great Landslide Case: Three Versions,* ed. Frank Anderson and Edgar M. Branch. The *Call* version (from an August 20, 1863, letter) is relatively brief and devoid of dialect. The original (actual) names of the participants are retained; the hoax and Roop's decision are presented in a simple, straightforward way. The Buffalo *Express* version is much longer and more elaborate. Sides gives a lengthy description (in hilarious dialect) of the avalanche and its effects; a detailed account is given of the courtroom speech and manner of Bunker (now called "Buncombe"); and Roop's speech is considerably expanded. The *Roughing It* version is based on the *Express* version, with a few relatively minor changes. The

most interesting change is that the plaintiff, Sides, is now called Hyde. The editors conjecture that Twain is poking fun at Mormon judge Orson Hyde, who, involved in a property dispute with Sides, had called down the judgment of God upon Sides (24–27).

21. *Roughing It,* 631–32, nn. 221.11–15; 632, nn. 223.18–19. Anderson and Branch suggest that heavy rains in early 1862 may have caused gravel and sand from Rust's (Morgan's) ranch to cover part of Sides's (Hyde's) ranch, though clearly there was no avalanche of the magnitude Twain depicts. At any rate, the episode lent itself to joking, and a mock trial somewhat akin to that presented in Twain's anecdote probably did occur in Carson City in February 1862 (Twain, *Great Landslide Case,* 19–24).

22. The editors contend that Twain may be lampooning, "through the metaphor of Judge Roop's unalterable 'monstrous decision,' the arbitrary, unreasonable nature of a fundamentalist God, Mormon or Puritan, whose word was law simply because it was His word." The self-righteous ranting of Mormon judge Orson Hyde and the puritanical Bunker would have been implicitly satirized. It is also suggested that Twain may have been satirizing the land-jumping that was so common in Nevada Territory just a few years earlier (Twain, *Great Landslide Case,* 20, 27).

23. Wadlington, *Confidence Game,* 205.

24. Editorial introduction, Twain, *Sandwich Islands,* x.

25. In their explanatory notes to *Roughing It,* the editors observe that Greeley was "one of Mark Twain's favorite targets for good-humored satire." The illegible letter satirized here was probably based on a May 7, 1871, letter that Greeley sent in response to Twain's lampooning of Greeley's book on agriculture (608–9, n. 131.12; 728, n. 484.17; 794–95, Supplement C). Bridgman, *Traveling in Twain,* 41.

26. Bridgman, *Traveling in Twain,* 42.

27. Bruce Michelson, "Ever Such a Good Time: The Structure of Mark Twain's *Roughing It,*" 183, 186, 190–92, 195–97.

28. Hill, "Mark Twain's *Roughing It,*" 9.

29. Beidler, "Realistic Style," 40.

Bibliography

❦

Beidler, Philip D. "Realistic Style and the Problem of Context in *The In-nocents Abroad* and *Roughing It.*" *American Literature* 52 (1980–1981): 33–49.

Bellamy, Gladys. *Mark Twain as a Literary Artist.* Norman: University of Oklahoma Press, 1950.

Benson, Ivan. *Mark Twain's Western Years.* Stanford: Stanford University Press, 1938.

Bergson, Henri. *Laughter: An Essay on the Meaning of the Comic.* Trans. Cloudesley Brereton and Fred Rothwell. New York: Macmillan, 1937.

Billington, Ray Allen. *Land of Savagery, Land of Promise.* Norman: University of Oklahoma Press, 1981.

Blair, Walter. *Horse Sense in American Literature.* Chicago: University of Chicago Press, 1942.

———. *Native American Humor.* New York: American Book, 1937.

Blair, Walter, and Hamlin Hill. *America's Humor: From Poor Richard to Doonesbury.* New York: Oxford University Press, 1978.

Booth, Wayne C. *The Rhetoric of Fiction.* 2d ed. Chicago: University of Chicago Press, 1983.

———. *A Rhetoric of Irony.* Chicago: University of Chicago Press, 1974.

Brackman, Jacob. *The Put-on: Modern Fooling and Modern Mistrust.* Chicago: Henry Regnery, 1971.

Branch, Edgar M. "Fact and Fiction in the Blind Lead Episode of *Roughing It.*" *Nevada Historical Society Quarterly* 28 (winter 1985): 234–48.

———. *The Literary Apprenticeship of Mark Twain.* Urbana: University of Illinois Press, 1950.

Bridgman, Richard. *Traveling in Mark Twain.* Berkeley and Los Angeles: University of California Press, 1987.

Brooks, Van Wyck. *The Ordeal of Mark Twain.* New York: E. P. Dutton, 1920.

Budd, Louis. "Mark Twain Talks Mostly about Humor and Humorists." *Studies in American Humor* 1 (April 1974): 4–22.

———. *Our Mark Twain.* Philadelphia: University of Pennsylvania Press, 1983.

Burns, Philip. "Fabrication and Faultline: Language as Experience in *Roughing It." Midwest Quarterly* 29:2 (winter 1988): 249–63.

Campbell, Joseph. *The Hero with a Thousand Faces.* 2d ed. Princeton: Princeton University Press, 1968.

Covici, Pascal, Jr. *Mark Twain's Humor: The Image of a World.* Dallas: Southern Methodist University Press, 1962.

Cox, James M. *Mark Twain: The Fate of Humor.* Princeton: Princeton University Press, 1966.

DeVoto, Bernard. *Mark Twain's America.* Boston: Little, Brown, 1932.

Dickinson, Leon T. "Mark Twain's Revisions in Writing *The Innocents Abroad." American Literature* 19 (1947–1948): 139–57.

Duncan, Jeffrey L. "The Empirical and the Ideal in Mark Twain." *PMLA* 95 (1980): 201–12.

Emerson, Everett. *The Authentic Mark Twain.* Philadelphia: University of Pennsylvania Press, 1984.

Ensor, Allison. *Mark Twain and the Bible.* Lexington: University of Kentucky Press, 1969.

Fatout, Paul. *Mark Twain in Virginia City.* Bloomington: Indiana University Press, 1964.

Fender, Stephen. "'The Prodigal in a Far Country Chawing of Husks': Mark Twain's Search for a Style in the West." *Modern Language Review* 71 (1976): 737–56.

Ferguson, DeLancey. *Mark Twain: Man and Legend.* Indianapolis: Bobbs-Merrill, 1943.

Fiedler, Leslie. Afterword to *The Innocents Abroad,* by Mark Twain. New York: New American Library, 1966.

Freud, Sigmund. "Humour." In *The Standard Edition of the Complete Psychological Works of Sigmund Freud,* ed. and trans. James Strachey, 21:159–66. London: Hogarth Press, 1961.

Ganzel, Dewey. *Mark Twain Abroad: The Cruise of the "Quaker City."* Chicago: University of Chicago Press, 1968.

Gerber, John C. "Mark Twain's Use of the Comic Pose." *PMLA* 77 (1962): 297–304.

Gibson, William M. *The Art of Mark Twain.* New York: Oxford University Press, 1976.

Gribben, Alan. *Mark Twain's Library.* 2 vols. Boston: G. K. Hall, 1980.

Hardison, O. B., Jr. *Disappearing through the Skylight.* New York: Penguin Books, 1990.

Hauck, Richard. *A Cheerful Nihilism: Confidence and "The Absurd" in American Humorous Fiction.* Bloomington: Indiana University Press, 1971.

Hill, Hamlin. "Mark Twain's *Roughing It:* The End of the American Dream." In *Proceedings of the Second University of Wyoming American Studies Conference: American Renaissance and American West,* ed. Christopher S. Durer et al., 3–13. Laramie: University of Wyoming Press, 1982.

Holland, Norman N. *Laughing: A Psychology of Humor.* Ithaca: Cornell University Press, 1982.

Howells, William Dean. *My Mark Twain: Reminiscences and Criticism.* Ed. Marilyn Austin Baldwin. Baton Rouge: Louisiana State University Press, 1967.

Huizinga, Johan. *Homo Ludens.* Boston: Beacon Press, 1950.

Kahn, Sholom J. *Mark Twain's "Mysterious Stranger": A Study of the Manuscript Texts.* Columbia: University of Missouri Press, 1978.

Kaplan, Justin. *Mr. Clemens and Mark Twain.* New York: Simon and Schuster, 1966.

Karnath, David. "Mark Twain's Implicit Theory of the Comic." *Mosaic* 9 (summer 1978): 207–18.

Kaufman, William. "The Comedic Stance: Sam Clemens, His Masquerade." In *Mark Twain: A Sumptuous Variety,* ed. Robert Giddings, 77–107. London: Vision Press, 1985.

Kierkegaard, Søren. *The Concept of Irony.* Ed. and trans. Howard V. Hong and Edna H. Hong. Princeton: Princeton University Press, 1989.

Kolb, Harold H., Jr. "Mark Twain and the Myth of the West." In *The Mythologizing of Mark Twain,* ed. Sara de Saussure Davis and Philip Beidler, 119–35. Birmingham: University of Alabama Press, 1984.

Kosinski, Mark. "Mark Twain's Absurd Universe and 'The Great Dark.'" *Studies in Short Fiction* 16 (1979): 335–40.

Lynn, Kenneth S. *Mark Twain and Southwestern Humor.* Boston: Little, Brown, 1959.

Macnaughton, William. *Mark Twain's Last Years as a Writer.* Columbia: University of Missouri Press, 1979.

Marx, Leo. *The Machine in the Garden.* New York: Oxford University Press, 1967.

McCloskey, John C. "Mark Twain as Critic in *The Innocents Abroad.*" *American Literature* 25 (1953): 139–51.

Michelson, Bruce. "Ever Such a Good Time: The Structure of Mark Twain's *Roughing It.*" *Dutch Quarterly Review of Anglo-American Letters* 17:3 (1987): 182–99.

———. "Mark Twain the Tourist: The Form of *The Innocents Abroad.*" *American Literature* 49 (1977): 385–98.

Mitchell, Lee Clark. "Verbally *Roughing It:* The West of Words." *Nineteenth-Century Literature* 44 (1989–1990): 67–92.

Regan, Robert. "The Reprobate Elect in *The Innocents Abroad.*" *American Literature* 54 (1982–1983): 240–57.

Robinson, Forrest G. "Patterns of Consciousness in *The Innocents Abroad.*" *American Literature* 58 (1986): 46–63.

Rogers, Franklin R. *Mark Twain's Burlesque Patterns.* Dallas: Southern Methodist University Press, 1960.

Rourke, Constance. *American Humor.* New York: Harcourt, Brace, 1931.

Salomon, Roger. *Twain and the Image of History.* New Haven: Yale University Press, 1961.

Sewell, David R. *Mark Twain's Languages: Discourse, Dialogue, and Linguistic Variety.* Berkeley and Los Angeles: University of California Press, 1987.

Sloane, David E. E. *Mark Twain as a Literary Comedian.* Baton Rouge: Louisiana State University Press, 1979.

Smith, Henry Nash. *Mark Twain: The Development of a Writer.* Cambridge: Harvard University Press, 1962.

———. "Mark Twain as Interpreter of the West: The Structure of *Roughing It.*" In *The Frontier in Perspective,* ed. Walker D. Wyman and Clifton B. Kroeber, 205–28. Madison: University of Wisconsin Press, 1957.

———. *Mark Twain's Fable of Progress.* New Brunswick: Rutgers University Press, 1964.

———. *Virgin Land.* Cambridge: Harvard University Press, 1950.

Steinbrink, Jeffrey. *Getting to Be Mark Twain.* Berkeley and Los Angeles: University of California Press, 1991.

Tandy, Jennette. *Crackerbox Philosophers in American Humor and Satire.* New York: Columbia University Press, 1925.

Towers, Tom. "'Hateful Reality': The Failure of the Territory in *Roughing It.*" *Western American Literature* 9 (1974): 3–15.

Twain, Mark. *Clemens of the "Call."* Ed. Edgar M. Branch. Berkeley and Los Angeles: University of California Press, 1969.

———. *Contributions to the "Galaxy," 1868–1871.* Ed. Bruce R. McElderry Jr. Gainesville, Fla.: Scholars' Facsimiles and Reprints, 1961.

———. *Early Tales and Sketches.* Vols. 1, 2 (1851–1864, 1864–1865). Ed. Edgar M. Branch and Robert H. Hirst. Vol. 15 of *The Works of Mark Twain,* ed. Frederick Anderson and Robert H. Hirst. Berkeley and Los Angeles: University of California Press, 1979, 1981.

———. *The Great Landslide Case: Three Versions.* Ed. Frank Anderson and Edgar M. Branch. Berkeley: Friends of the Bancroft Library, 1972.

———. *The Innocents Abroad.* Ed. Guy Cardwell. New York: Literary Classics of the United States, 1984.

———. *Letters from the Sandwich Islands.* Ed. G. Ezra Dane. Stanford: Stanford University Press, 1938.

———. *Mark Twain of the "Enterprise."* Ed. Henry Nash Smith and Frederick Anderson. Berkeley and Los Angeles: University of California Press, 1957.

———. *Mark Twain's Notebooks and Journals.* Vol. 1 (1855–1873). Ed. Frederick Anderson, Michael B. Frank, and Kenneth M. Sanderson. No. 8 in *The Mark Twain Papers,* ed. Frederick Anderson. Berkeley and Los Angeles: University of California Press, 1975.

———. *Mark Twain's Travels with Mr. Brown.* Ed. Franklin Walker and G. Ezra Dane. New York: Alfred A. Knopf, 1940.

———. *The Pattern for Mark Twain's "Roughing It."* Ed. Franklin R. Rogers. Berkeley and Los Angeles: University of California Press, 1961.

———. *Roughing It.* Ed. Harriet Elinor Smith, Edgar Marquess Branch, Lin Salamo, and Robert Pack Browning. Vol. 2 of *The Works of Mark Twain,* ed. Robert H. Hirst. Berkeley and Los Angeles: University of California Press, 1993.

———. *Traveling with the Innocents Abroad.* Ed. Daniel Morley McKeithan. Norman: University of Oklahoma Press, 1958.

———. *The Washoe Giant in San Francisco.* Ed. Franklin Walker. San Francisco: George Fields, 1938.

Wadlington, Warwick. *The Confidence Game in American Literature.* Princeton: Princeton University Press, 1975.

Wagenknecht, Edward. *Mark Twain: The Man and His Work.* Rev. ed. Norman: University of Oklahoma Press, 1961.

Walker, Franklin. *Irreverent Pilgrims: Melville, Browne, and Mark Twain in the Holy Land.* Seattle: University of Washington Press, 1974.

Wecter, Dixon. *Sam Clemens of Hannibal.* Boston: Houghton Mifflin, 1952.

Williams, George, III. *Mark Twain: His Adventures at Aurora and Mono Lake.* Dayton, Nev.: Tree by the River Publishing, 1986.

———. *Mark Twain: His Life in Virginia City, Nevada.* Riverside, Calif.: Tree by the River Publishing, 1985.

Wilson, James C. "'The Great Dark': Invisible Spheres, Formed in Fright." *Midwest Quarterly* 23:2 (winter 1982): 229–43.

Index